Seeking God's Truth in a Troubled World

(36 Devotional Meditations for Honest Truth Seekers)

Richard Williams

Parson's Porch Books

Seeking God's Truth in a Troubled World
ISBN: Softcover 978-1-960326-49-2

Parson's Porch Books is an imprint of Parson's Porch *&* Company (PP*&*C) in Cleveland, Tennessee. PP*&*C is a self-funded charity which earns money by publishing books of noted authors, representing all genres. Its face and voice is **David Russell Tullock** (dtullock@parsonsporch.com).

Parson's Porch *&* Company *turns books into bread & milk* by sharing its profits with the poor.

www.parsonsporch.com

Seeking God's Truth in a Troubled World

Contents

Dedication

To my three beautiful daughters, Leslie, Tonja, and Allison, who have inspired me to be the best father I could be and have caused me to cry out to Jesus for wisdom and compassion.

Memorial

To Nick and Mark, two sons called home far too early for their mother and me. Although you are no longer in our presence, your light will forever shine in our hearts,

Foreword

I have known Richard and walked with him in ministry for more than thirty years; I've seen the joys and sorrows, the ups and downs, and the successes and failures of a life well lived. It is out of his life's journey that Richard shares this inspiring and challenging book. Everything in it is authentically drawn from the experiences of his own life that have made him into the loving father, faithful friend, and Christian leader that he is today.

Through the challenges of a near-death experience with Covid-19, stage 4 cancer, and deep personal loss, Richard has made his relationship with Jesus priority. When asked how deep one can really go in their relationship with God, his profound response is: *"there is no bottom."* But at the same time, Richard is quick to acknowledge that through the tough times of life, maintaining the closeness of that relationship with Jesus has not been without a struggle. It is that struggle that makes this book both profound and yet simple. It comes from deep within his heart through keen perception and careful thought.

Richard has always been a storyteller. This book is the story of his life. But not just his life. More importantly, it is the story of his walk with God. As he shares his life-story, he admits, *"much of my life was spent chasing my own desires while at the same time wanting to know that I was doing what God would have me do."* In this story you may find parts of your story. You might laugh. You might cry. You might disagree. But you will be touched. You will be inspired. And you will be challenged.

One cannot be around Richard very long without seeing the depth of his love and compassion for others. Vivid are the scenes in my memory of Richard caring for "the least of these." One of those vivid scenes is of a cold blustery day in Chester, Pennsylvania, just outside Philadelphia. A mother came into the mission building with a cold and crying little girl, probably not more than eight years old. The little girl's shoes were in taters, her clothes filthy and ragged, her face streaked as tears flowed down her dirty face. Richard didn't call one of his staff. He didn't give a cloth and water to the mother. He didn't hesitate for a moment. He picked up that little girl and sat her on the counter next to the sink. After removing her tattered shoes, he took soap and a warm wet cloth and gently washed her cold filthy feet, all the while speaking softly to the child. The scene is forever etched in my mind as I was reminded of Jesus' act of compassion and humility when He washed the disciples' feet. That's my image of Jesus. That's my image of Richard Williams.

Richard's compassion and concern for people is evident not only as he cares for the physical needs, but also as he cares about their spiritual life and future. That's why he wrote this book. And it is because of that love and compassion that the message of this book will touch your heart. It's an important message for our time from the heart of a caring and honest fellow-traveler, encouraging us all to stay on the *straight and narrow* road that leads to a life of joy and fulfilment, and an eternity with Jesus that will surpass anything we could possibly imagine.

However, you should not read this book unless you are prepared to have some of your cherished faith-beliefs challenged. Although packed with Scripture, it is not a theological treatise. This book feels more like a heartfelt chat with an old friend – someone who has walked with Jesus for a long time and is passionate about being what God wants him to be. It is biblically sound, taking sometimes complex themes and sharing simple, profound, livable truth. In this book, Richard is willing to tackle some of the most complex and challenging questions of life. He is not afraid to ask himself (and us as readers) the difficult and challenging questions. "*Will the fact that I have spent over seventy years on earth thus far mean anything? Will my time on earth have made a difference, or will it just be time spent not doing bad things, maybe even some good things, but having no lasting impact on those left behind? Is it possible in this life to really be like Christ? What would I want my tombstone to say?"*

In *"Seeking God's Truth in a Troubled World,"* Richard takes some of the most common biblical themes and shares a perspective that comes from deep within his heart – a heart that is in tune with the Father and desires more than anything to serve Him to the end. But please don't miss Richard's central theme – Jesus, and the fullness of the salvation He offers to everyone. So, take your time as you read. Let the message, through the gentle urging of the Holy Spirit, sink deep within your soul bringing refreshment and nourishment along your life-journey. You won't be disappointed.

David F. Hunt, DMin

Endorsements

If you are seeking a book that goes beyond first principles, this book is for you. If you are seeking a devotional book that not only inspires but also teaches deeper truth regarding Godly living, this book is for you. In his book, "Seeking God's Truth in a Troubled World" Richard covers a plethora of subjects from fear, anxiety, forgiveness, prayer, plus many other pertinent subjects.

As you read this, you will realize Godly change results when we surrender completely to God. And once we are surrendered, and the old nature is crucified, we begin walking in the Spirit and Christlikeness ensues.

Carl E. Roberts
Retired Pharmacist/Sunday School Teacher

I loved this book! Richard has taken a very honest and direct approach in showing us what Jesus did, as well as what He tells us to do.

The premise of the book is based on a solid foundation of Scripture which should not be debated. He also addresses the provisions in which God has given to us that enable us to live holy and Godly lives. Maybe just importantly Richard shows us ways in which we are to love Jesus.

These are 36 powerful chapters in which Jesus is brought to bear in all of them. I see this book in light of the Kingdom of God. Kingdom is a word that is rarely used by the church today, yet Jesus used it all the time. If we are true believers we understand that we are living in the Kingdom now and not in some distant future when we die.

Richard has brought honesty and clarity to the Scriptures contained in the 36 chapters of this book. These are passages that represent well the wisdom of Jesus in the Scriptures.

Jerry Trousdale
Past President Final Command
Author, "Miraculous Movements" and "The Kingdom Unleashed"

I couldn't put the book down. Thank you for being so transparent. It is a book that I wanted to race through, getting more and more excited with each page. I found myself saying "ouch" every few pages. (But it is an "ouch" with hope and inspiration attached by the Holy Spirit that "yes, you can do this, with my help"). Now, I just want to take each devotional slowly, perhaps over several days or more, and ponder and pray, and live it out in obedience. Richard's book is so refreshing, and very encouraging. He carries the heart of God. It is written in a very conversational style, like he is sitting down and talking to you across the kitchen table. May it draw thirsty people from all walks and stages of life, and give them a long, cool, drink of living water they won't forget.

Marty and Elaine Mattocks
DMM practitioners and trainers
Asia Highland Partners, Board Advisors

The author shares from his lifelong passion and dedication to serving our Almighty God. In this revealing account of a life lived out through Jesus Christ, you will be challenged to explore the depth of God's power available to all of us. Richard shares from his own lifetime of experience just how deep in God's love we can all live. The truths of these devotionals about God's grace should be proclaimed to the ends of the earth.

Robert Reid, Retired
SMSGT, USAF

In Richard's book 'Seeking God's Truth in a Troubled World" we get a glimpse of his transparency and his walk with God. We see God's sovereignty and His fingerprints over his life. His love for people is evident in his book, as he seeks God, obeys God, and wants to pass on this treasure to his readers. His desire to please His master shows in every word he writes, as is his desire to pass that on to others. He truly goes to the heart of having a personal relationship with the Creator in showing the reader "The Truth of God's Word". His heart and love for God are evident as he wants to see everyone come to the saving knowledge of Jesus Christ.. He points out that this can only happen by having an intimate relationship with the Master. So read, soak in God, surrender all, and begin a richer relationship with the God of the universe. Richard's book has affirmed within me that I am truly a daughter of the King, and a sister to His son, Jesus Christ.

Rachel Kent, Prayer Coordinator
Compassion for Life

We all need help, support, inspiration, and direction in our Christian walk today!! You will find it in this book. Short, and to the point, only 36 quick reads.

With some 50 years of Christian ministry behind him, and the Holy Spirit's inspiration, Reverend Richard Williams produced a special message in every chapter that you will find gratifying and useful, as well as encouraging.

Richard and I have worked together for some 35 years starting when he came to work for Cityteam Ministries in Chester, PA.. Chester brings out your Christianity very quickly or you leave the city. Having worked with him down in the trenches and at the Board of Directors level, I know he exemplifies what it is to truly follow Jesus Christ.

God has blessed Richard's Christian journey with many different experiences, but the most important one is that he has shown so many the way to salvation through Jesus Christ.

May God bless you and enrich your life as you read this book.

Joseph N. Pew, President
Pew Dingfelder Corp.

The Word of God is living as the "sword of the Spirit" and. therefore, will do remarkable things in our lives, if we let it. My dear friend and colleague, Richard Williams, has helpfully shared intimate details of his life as he grew to embrace, over time and through many trials, how the Lord has challenged, changed, and blessed him through yielding his life and obeying the eternal Word. This book is simply worth reading because its 36 brilliant text and topics will challenge, change and bless you-if that is the longing of your heart.

Dr. Ed Gross, DMis
Compassion for Life

This is an incredible book! Not only does it provide a glimpse into the life of the writer, his upbringing, maturing, and spiritual work, but it also inspires one to ponder over what happens after death. The writer encourages us to prepare ourselves for the afterlife. It is reassuring in that it speaks to the question of faith in which Christians can be certain that having faithfully served the good Lord, there should be no fear when death comes knocking at the door. This is a piece of work that will live to inspire generations of Christians. I believe that it is a ministry in itself that has the potential to change minds and encourage believers and non-believers facing challenges of health and social imperatives.

Deacon George S.W. Patten, Sr.
Former Ambassador of the Republic of Liberia to the United
States, Canada, and Mexico

This is a book you simply must read if you desire to go deeper, much deeper in your walk with Jesus. Richard takes you through his thought process in evaluating his relationship with God. "Seeking God's Truth in a Troubled World" will help you evaluate your own relationship with the Creator of the World. Let Richard lead your thinking into places that you haven't given much thought until now. You will grow in your relationship with Christ as a result.

Richard, thank you for your thoughtful guidance, and sharing your personal story about seeking Jesus.

Judy and Bill Strine
Media, PA.

Viewed through his lens of real world experiences, Richard leads us on an honest, insightful, and candid journey into the heart of a Pastor and disciple-maker. He openly shares the triumphs, the struggles, as well as the failures that have shaped his life. He shares that obedience is the key to a closer walk with our Lord and Savior.

The author does not shy away from letting us know that on this side of eternity life will be challenging. "Seeking God's Truth in a Troubled World" provides practical, Biblical principles that lead Christ followers into intimate fellowship with the God who created us. Richard is a true disciple of Jesus Christ, and through the pages of his book he shares his deepest desire. That is for everyone who professes to be a Christian, that they will enjoy a deep intimate relationship with Christ, and not just a religious experience. Living in obedience to God's word, and compelled by gratitude and love, he seeks to bring honor and glory to Christ.

Bruce W. Cobb

Master Chief Navy Counselor, Retired

Acknowledgements

To Mike Boling who without him this book would never have been written. You came into my life when I was a very angry, bitter young man. I was mad at the world and especially at God and many so-called Christians. Without ever preaching at me or condemning my behavior you patiently befriended me and accepted me for who I was. Your life was the best sermon I had ever heard. I watched you live out your faith waiting for any opportunity to find fault with who you claimed to be. It would be the life you lived that would eventually break my hard exterior and lead me to Christ. What you possessed was real, and I wanted the peace that was in your life. You faced many of the same challenges in life that I had faced and instead of being filled with anger and doubt, you were rock solid in your trust of God. I hungered for what I saw in you. You were a Christian in more than words. You lived it out and guided me to start my own journey into a trusting relationship with Jesus Christ.

To Dave Hunt, who has been my partner in ministry for over thirty years. I have learned more about leadership from you than all the books on management that I have read, as well as all the seminars I attended over the years. We both laugh when I credit you for showing me where the keyboard was located on my computer. Partnering together we have successfully completed two start-up ministries, worked with overseas missions, and trained a host of other missionaries and church planters with the knowledge I gained throughout the years. It is only you that I have trusted to read the manuscript and give me your honest and critical opinion on the content. Whatever success I have achieved in ministry has to be in part credited to the relationship that we share.

Introduction

It was sometime in 2021, my wife was taking care of her mother after a fall that had broken her hip. I found myself alone having lunch in a restaurant as a result. While waiting on my order to arrive, I began to take inventory of my life over the past few years. There were years that saw dramatic changes in my life. I had left a ministry that I had devoted thirty-five years of my life to. I had surgery for stage four prostate cancer, to be followed by six days in ICU with Covid 19. All of this while starting a new non-profit ministry. If you have ever done a start-up, you know the many hours it takes of filing government papers, creating budgets, deciding the direction of the ministry, recruiting staff, as well as finding ways to communicate to supporters why I needed to start a new organization after thirty-five fruitful years at a prior one.

I pulled out my Bible while waiting for my order to arrive. I love the Psalms and decided I would read a few for a little encouragement. I came across Psalms 71:18-23 NLT: *"Now that I am old and gray, do not abandoned me O God. Let me proclaim your power to this new generation, your mighty miracles for all who come after me. Your righteousness, O God, reaches to the highest heavens. You have done such wonderful things. Who can compare with you, O God? You have allowed me to suffer much hardship, but you will restore me to life again and lift me up from the depths of the earth. You will restore me to even greater honor and comfort once again. Then I will praise you with music on the harp because you are faithful to your promises. O my God, I will sing praises to you with a lyre, O Holy One from Israel. I will shout for joy and sing your praises, for you have ransomed me."*

That was the beginning of what would eventually become this book. As I sat there, I began to wonder how much of a difference I had made with my life up to this point. I could think of a few things that I felt were worthwhile, but at the same time there were many more failures along the way as well. What did others think of me as a Christian? I wondered if my co-workers saw me as kind and Christlike, or did they see more of the human side of me. Most important to me was how my children viewed me up to this point. Did they see me through a lens of failures and mistakes, or did they see Christ living within my heart and soul?

That is when I began to write. At first it was more journaling and saving my thoughts for my children and grandchildren. I decided to share some of my writings with a few close friends both for feedback on content, as well as for affirmation that I was Biblically correct. Eventually I began posting some of them on Facebook. I was surprised at the many positive responses I began to receive, especially those encouraging me to write this book.

All in all, this book is a compilation of my personal thoughts I wanted to say to my family, especially my children, as well as many personal experiences. Most important of all, this book is about a journey I have been on for fifty plus years, going deep into a spiritual relationship with God through His Son Jesus Christ. I was asked recently by one of the persons endorsing this book, "How deep can you really go in a relationship with God?" My answer was simple and yet I hope profound: "there is no bottom!"

There is no chronology or particular order to the chapters. You may want to look for and read chapters that speak to what you may be experiencing at the time. I encourage you to stop after you read a chapter and ponder what it may mean to your current situation. Or perhaps you may choose to read one chapter a week, or to re-read a chapter two or three times during a week, or during a time where a given chapter speaks to your heart and need at the moment. In any case, I pray that as you read about the various subjects I write about, that you find a few answers to questions you may have pondered in your own life. Most importantly, I pray that it makes you hunger to go deep in your relationship with Jesus Christ.

Some of the chapters in the book first appeared on my social media. These postings were inserted into the book in their original format. The post invited people to contact me with questions or to discuss how those chapters could apply to their lives. I have left that invitation in the book and extend it to you the reader.

Scripture passages were all from the New Living Translation unless otherwise noted.

Chapter 1

Legacy

"Now that I am old and gray, do not abandon me oh God. Let me proclaim your power to this new generation, Your mighty miracles to all who come after me" (Psalm 71:18).

Life for me began to change in 2015. Prior to that I had never seen the inside of a hospital room. That is, not as a patient. It was in the winter of that year that I was diagnosed with stage 4 prostate cancer. Now, I had always heard that prostate cancer was very slow growing, so you can imagine my surprise when the oncologist told me that any treatment short of a radical prostatectomy would mean three to six months to live. It is now eight years later, and God has shown me His grace. Doctors now tell me I have a ninety-six percent survival rate.

Fast forward to 2020 and Covid-19 is running rampant throughout the world. Once again, I am not exempt from its possibility of death. When first diagnosed I didn't believe it. It must be a false positive because I just didn't feel that bad. Forty-eight hours later I would be convinced. I was so weak I could not raise my head from my pillow, I could not get breath, and my pulse had fallen to the mid-80s and below. Still, I was determined I could beat this on my own and refused to go to the hospital. It wasn't until my wife fell apart crying beside my bed that I relinquished and allowed her to take me to the emergency room. I thought, "Okay, they will give me an antibiotic and send me home." Six days later I did go home, but recovery would take the better part of a year. In some areas I still have not recovered.

Three months ago, while on a West Coast trip I was feeling bad and presumed once again that it is "just" a cold. I finished my meetings and caught my flight home. My breathing became shallow and no matter how hard I tried I could barely inhale or exhale. Upon landing I knew I was in trouble and immediately arranged to see my primary care doctor. It was discovered that my lungs were covered in blood clots – a result of either the Covid itself, or the vaccines.

I have reached that season of life in which I am faced with realizing my own mortality. By God's grace I have escaped death not once, or twice, but three times. However, the time is coming in the not-so-distant future when my time on earth will be done. As the writer of Hebrews said, *"It is appointed unto man once to die."* David said while fearing for his life, *"there is but a step between me and death"* (1 Samuel 20:3). Thanks to Christ, for those who put their faith and trust in Him, earthly death is not the end but the beginning of our real life with Him in Heaven.

So why am I writing about this? One reason only - legacy. Will the fact that I have spent over 70 years on earth thus far mean anything? As I write this it is Memorial Day, 2023 - a day we remember loved ones gone on before us. I am currently down in my home state of Arkansas. Yesterday I was invited to attend a family reunion of my brother-in-law's family. I felt honored to be invited and to see everyone that I met at my sister's funeral a few years ago. I sat and listened as different ones talked about loved ones who had gone on before them. Some I knew, others only from the stories I heard. It was heart-warming as each person spoke with love and kindness about their family members.

On the drive home I couldn't help but think of what people would say about me once my time on earth is over. More importantly, will my time on earth have made a difference? Or will it just be time spent maybe not doing anything bad, maybe even some good things, but no lasting impact on those left behind? What will my legacy be?

I pray that the way in which I have lived my life would be reflected in my children and grandchildren. Perhaps something that I have said, or the way I have approached life by loving God would become a part of their DNA. I pray that they will have the same hunger for the things of God that I have had in my life.

I also think of the many paths of people that I have crossed throughout the years. Will their interaction with me be soon forgotten once I am gone, or will I have left some little part of me with them? Did they learn from me in understanding the difference in knowing about God, and in knowing God? Most importantly, did others see Jesus in me? If the answer to any of this is no, then I have failed.

Let me share with you a poem I picked up some years ago that explains it all. Perhaps you have heard of it. It is called *"The Dash"* by Linda Ellis.

I read of a man who stood to speak at the funeral of a friend.
He referred to the dates on the tombstone from the beginning - to the end.
He noted that first came the date of birth and spoke of the following date with tears.
But he said what mattered most of all was the dash between those years.
For that dash represents all the time they spent alive on earth.
And now only those who loved them know what that little line is worth.
For it matters not how much we own, the cars, the house, the cash.
What matters is how we live and love and how we spend our dash.
So, think about this long and hard; are there things you'd like to change?
For you never know how much time is left that still can be rearranged.
To be less quick to anger and show appreciation more,
And love the people in our lives like we've never loved before.
If we treat each other with respect and more often wear a smile,
Remembering that this special dash might only last a little while.
So, when your eulogy is being read, with your life's actions to rehash,
Would you be proud of the things they say about how you lived your dash?

On my way home from the reunion I had been invited to, I took a little detour. I stopped by the cemetery where all my family is buried. While there I found myself walking around reading some of the epitaphs on different tombstones. One read "loving father and husband," one child's marker read, "our little ray of sunshine, taken too soon." I began to think, *what would I want my tombstone to say?* I would hope it would be true to say something like, "well done my faithful servant."

Chapter 2

The Power That Accompanies Salvation

"Work hard to show the results of your salvation, obeying God with deep reverence and fear. For God is working in you giving you the desire and the power to do what pleases Him" (Philippians 2:12b, 13).

Working hard to show the results of our salvation is not something that most Christians want to talk about. We live in a day and age where we are led to believe that all that is necessary to be *saved* is to just say a *sinner's prayer* and that is it. At best this form of *easy believing* will produce weak, anemic Christians that never experience the power that can accompany salvation. They will struggle through life with their faith challenged during every crisis of life. Many will *fall away* like seeds scattered on stony ground. Shortly after 9/11, I had a board member come to me and resign. She couldn't put her faith in a God who would let this happen. She never experienced the power of salvation and when faced with this adversity was driven away from the very God that could give her the power to overcome not only this but any other evil that could be thrown at her.

We are told that we must do two things in this life once we have received salvation:

1. Work hard
2. Be obedient with reverence and fear.

Obeying God is a subject that most people, even Christians don't like to talk about anymore. Yet you cannot read one single book of the Bible from Genesis to Revelation without seeing an underlying theme of obedience.

However, we should not look at obedience to God as something I *have* to do, but as something I am motivated to do out of appreciation for His sacrifice on the Cross on my behalf. Listen to the way Paul phrases his words: *"obeying God with deep <u>reverence</u> and <u>fear</u>."* When I first became a Christian and I read those words, I didn't like what I read. I didn't want to serve God out of fear. I even looked it up in the Greek thinking surely it meant something similar to what it means in Acts which actually means *awe*. I could accept serving Him with reverence and awe. My hope for a more palatable definition was short lived. I discovered that here in this passage, fear means fear. I struggled for years thinking that I had to serve God out of fear.

As I have grown older, I have come to a deeper understanding of fear. It is a human emotion that we all possess, and our emotions have been woven into the DNA that God created us with. It is when we are not surrendering those emotions to God that they can become something negative. I will attempt to give an example of fear from a positive perspective. I have three beautiful daughters. When they were growing up, I had lots of fears. I feared that I would not be a good father and that I might fail to live my life in such a way that would draw them to Christ. When they were old enough to drive, I feared every time they got in the car, I feared their dating, going to parties, and their choice of friends. Yet it was these fears that caused me to want to be a good dad. My fear caused me to want to set a good example of a godly Father. I worked at teaching them to drive safely, how to choose friends wisely, and the dangers of drugs and alcohol. In other words, my fear motivated me to do good because I loved my children.

This is what Paul was talking about when he said, *"obey God with deep reverence and fear."* We obey God, not because we are afraid of Him, but rather because we have this deep respect and gratitude for His presence in our lives. The fear should be in the same context as the fears I had for my children: a fear of failing Him; a fear that if I do not live a godly life, I may turn others off from wanting to know Him; a fear that if I do not make myself available there will be those who may slip into eternity without Him. That type of fear is healthy. It motivates us to give our best to God. When we understand fear in that context then rather than being turned off by the thought of being obedient, we embrace it. Verse thirteen of Philippians 2 is actually a litmus test for us as believers. God is working in us *giving us the desire to please Him.*" The litmus test is this: do you have a desire to please Him? If not, we need to really consider if we have ever allowed Him into our lives in the first place. If we have, that desire should be evident to us. God has also given us the power and strength to obediently do whatever He ask of us. When we master the desire and the power, the fear will disappear, and we will know that God is pleased that we are serving Him from a place of deep reverence and healthy fear.

So, what does God desire of us? I have no clue what that may be for you. I am a slow learner, and it took me years to figure out what he desired of me. I can tell you that when you seriously seek Him out to show you what He desires of you, it will become very clear. The desire will lead you there.

So far, we have established that we are to work hard because of our salvation. The question immediately causes us to ask, "work hard at what?" This triggers what I have referred to as the litmus test. True believers have had implanted into them first a desire to please Him. If that desire is not present within you, you need to consider whether you have crucified the old nature and allowed God to give you a new nature, His nature. True believers have this burning desire to please God with everything they do. They simply cannot be pleased with the status quo of attending church, singing in the choir, or paying their tithe. They are driven, not by their own desires, but by His desires. The greatest example I could give would be for the very reason He came, suffered and died; He came to seek and save the lost. If there is no burden or desire to see the lost come to know Him, we really need to examine our heart to see if we have had a religious experience rather than a spiritual experience.

This leads me to the last part of this passage: the power to accomplish those desires of Christ. I, along with two of my closest spiritual mentors, have been studying about true Christlikeness. One of them asked, "do you realize that the same power that gave Jesus the power to be raised from the dead flows through our veins?" Hear Paul's statement in Philippians 3:10. *"I want to know Christ and experience the mighty power that raised Him from the dead."* Can you hear the urgency from Paul to possess the power of God? At this point in his life Paul's desires had changed from his own selfish desire to a desire to know and use the power of God that now flowed through His veins. The same power that Jesus possessed that allowed Him to see past what was on the outside of man and to see directly into their hearts. The same power that allowed Him to turn water into wine, to cause the blind to see, the deaf to hear, and the dead to be raised to life flows through the life of every true believer.

Are you using that power that is within you? Are you driven by the desires of God rather than your own? I end this with the words of Paul shortly after his Damascus Road experience in reference to power: *"I pray that God, the source of hope will fill you completely with joy and peace because you trust in Him. Then you will overflow with confident hope and through the power of the Holy Spirit."*

Chapter 3
Walking By Faith

"We walk by faith and not by sight" (2 Corinthians 5:7).

I actually like the New Living Translation of this one better than the King James Version. The NLT says it this way, *"We walk by believing not by seeing."* I'm not sure that even this translation gets to the heart of what the writer was trying to convey, but at least it gets us closer.

Faith is about believing that Christ is who He said He was and that He always has our best interest at heart. It is so easy to say that we believe or have faith in God when we are not faced with adversity in life. The real test of whether we really believe in God only comes when we are challenged with unexpected and unwelcomed events in our lives. I will write more about this in the chapter entitled *Doubt*, but for now I want to focus on the importance of trusting the Lord in every aspect of our lives and not just when things are going our way. I want to address two types of adversity that we go through in life that speaks to the importance of really believing with strong faith that nothing ever comes our way until it is first sifted through the divine fingers of God. Those two types are tragedy and uncertainty.

Tragedy
Let me give a disclaimer right up front. I do not know why certain tragedies occur in people's lives. I have sat with parents at the bedside of their dying children and have no answer for why their child was taken at the age of nine, ten, or eleven. I led a disaster team into Haiti several years ago and was faced with scenes that will never be erased from my mind: children whose limbs had been crushed by fallen debris, mothers holding in their arms infants that had been

crushed to death. Yes, I cried out to God like any human being would with a one-word question – WHY?! Why do some people have wealth and others do not have enough to buy food for their families? I could name a lot more instances of tragedy that people go through in their lives, but I think I have made the point that bad things happen to good people and on this side of heaven we will not have the answer as to why.

Counselors have a saying that I have come to use a lot, *circumstances will either make you bitter, or they will make you better*. It all depends on how we approach those times in our lives. In the spiritual sense, circumstances will either destroy our faith, or make it stronger. It is always our choice how we will respond. You can rest assured that when I get to heaven, I will ask the why questions and I am fully confident that God will have the answers we all seek. *"For now, we see in a mirror dimly, but then face to face. Now I know in part; then I shall fully know, even as I have been fully known"* (1 Corinthians 13:12).

Uncertainty

If you are facing uncertainty in your life, worried about your future, or not sure what decision to make regarding a life event that has serious implications, I offer you the following.

The King James Version says this: *"we walk by faith, not by sight."* My favorite translation says it this way, *"for we live by believing and not by seeing"* (NLT). The first time I read this Scripture in a meaningful way was in 1973. I had this strong sense from the Lord that I was to go to Bible College in Colorado Springs. Due to my practical way of thinking there was a huge battle of my mind vs. my heart. I called it war. This couldn't possibly be what God would want of me this late in my life. I was so troubled over it that I got up in the middle of the night to pray. It was more like me telling God all the practical reasons why I shouldn't go in hopes that He would be reasonable and leave me alone about it. Then I picked up my Bible and read those words, *"we walk by faith, not by sight."* I knew in that moment; I wasn't going to change His mind. So, with two kids and a wife, I quit my job, loaded up a Ryder truck and headed west. No job, no place to live, no savings to fall back on. Just enough faith to believe somehow, God would be enough. After a day and a half of driving I pulled into the school parking lot and went in to meet the school bursar, Mrs. Hubbard. She informed me that another married couple had agreed to allow us to stay with them until we could afford our own place. She handed me a list of employers that hired their students, told me I could pay for the first semester once I was employed, and sent me on my way. A week later I had a job as well as my own place to live. It wasn't much but it was enough, and I was beginning to be amazed about this God I had surrendered my *will* to. I had to apply for food stamps but ate better than I ever had in my life. I could have gotten use to that! It was hard that first semester. All my classes were in the morning. I would eat my sack lunch in my car on my way to work, work until close at 9:00 pm, drive thirty minutes home, eat a late dinner over my homework, go to bed, get up at 5 am and do it all over again. I tried saving money, but was just barely able to get by, much less save anything. By the end of semester, I finally realize that I cannot pay the back semester tuition much less pay for the second one. I would have to admit defeat, realize I was wrong to even do something this stupid and think it was *of God*. I informed Mrs. Hubbard I was withdrawing and apologized that I couldn't pay anything I owed. Imagine the look on my face when she just smiled at me for a moment and said, "Richard, someone has come forward to scholarship you throughout your time here. You are PAID IN FULL!" Here I am now after 47 years of serving the Lord full time, still *walking by faith and not by sight*. I could name a hundred times over the many times since then that God has amazed me. If you are reading this and struggling with fear with where you are in life, I promise that if you completely surrender to God and His will for you, He will amaze you too. *"I know the plans I have for you says the Lord. Plans for good and not disaster, plans to give you a future and a hope"* (Jeremiah 29:11).

Chapter 4
Fear and Anxiety

"Do not be afraid, for I am with you, do not be discouraged, for I am your God. I will strengthen you and help you. I will hold you up with my righteous right hand" (Isaiah 41:10).

Full disclosure...this is for me. If it speaks to you, we both win. That phrase, *"do not be afraid"* is found 366 times in the Bible. Someone said it is one for each day of the year plus one for leap year. You would think after walking with the Lord for fifty years I would have mastered this by now. I only wish that were the case. I have been here before and as I look back there has never been a time that God has failed me. I have no doubt in my mind that He will not fail me now. But, as in every case when life throws me a curve, I always suffer the anxiety until He delivers. So why am I telling you this tonight? One reason is to be transparent that I carry my faith in an earthen vessel that is far from perfect. Another reason is my sharing is good therapy for me to be brutally honest in my walk and witness; something that I have not always done in the past. I am just now learning the meaning of *"sharing your faults with one another"* and *"in your weakness you are made strong."*

I have many dear friends who have experienced tremendous pain and loss the last few years. I have watched as the grief and anxiety has taken them captive - far greater pain and loss than I have ever experienced to this point in my life. If you are suffering fear and anxiety in your life, as you read this, please know it doesn't mean you don't have enough faith. It simply means you are human and not able to see around the corner. God understands that.

Sometimes, as well-meaning Christians, we rush to judgement of others when they are struggling with fear or anxiety over some crisis in their lives. Several years ago, I lost a brother to kidney cancer. He had been diagnosed with a renal mass on his left kidney. Two years later I was diagnosed with a renal mass on my left kidney. My fear of dying a horrible death like my brother consumed me. In public I was the pillar of faith. However, behind closed doors I curled up in a fetal position and just tried to shut the world out. I read my Bible, prayed constantly, and listened to Christian music. I tried everything I could to push my fears away, but nothing worked. I wanted to be the spiritual man who God could count on to have the faith of Paul who said, *"to die is gain."* Instead, I cried real tears and begged God to let me live. Fortunately for me, He answered my prayer, and I am still here some fifteen-plus years later. However, I was ashamed of the fact that I allowed my fear of dying to control me. I am telling you this because I want you to know that God understands your fears. Just before Christ was to be crucified, He prayed a similar prayer to mine and asked the Father if there was any way possible to let *"this cup"* (death), pass from Him. At the same time, once we truly believe that God holds us in the palm of His hand, we truly can defeat those fears and anxiety that attack us in life.

In this passage, Israel was in captivity not knowing what was going to happen to them. He encourages them go on living, to marry, have children, and just put one foot in front of the other. They had no idea what God had in mind, or that He would deliver them. But God knew. Not only did He tell them to not be discouraged, but He promised to strengthen them, help them, and even hold them up with His hand. Let that sink in, God holding our hand like a father holding the hand of his little child. Many years ago in my youth, we used to sing a song, *"Many things about tomorrow, I don't seem to understand, but I know who holds the future, and I know who holds my hand."* When we are going through a dark valley, we may not know how long it will last, or how it will turn out, but God understands, and He has us by the hand.

My first cancer scare happened in about 2006 or 2007. I had another cancer diagnosis in 2015. This time it was stage four prostate cancer. I was told that it was too late to consider any type of treatment. Without a radical prostatectomy I would have no more than three to six months to live. It was different this time. God gifted me with what I can only describe as a peace that passes all understanding. I came across the following verses in Romans 14:7: *"If I live, I live as unto the Lord. If I die, I die as unto the Lord. So, whether I live, or whether I die, I belong to the Lord."* This has become a part of my DNA as His child. No matter what happens to me in this life, I realize that I belong to the Lord, and nothing will come my way that God can't handle on my behalf.

Psalm 37:7 says, *"Be still in the presence of the Lord and wait patiently for Him to act."* 1 Peter 5:7, *"Give all your cares and worries to God, for He cares for you."*

I have learned that if I will turn my fears and anxiety over to God; if I will just wait calmly - be still and patiently wait, God will give me the peace I need to overcome my fears.

"Tell God what you need and thank Him for what He has already done. <u>Then you will experience God's peace which exceeds anything we can understand. His peace will guard your heart and mind as you live in Christ Jesus</u> (Philippians 4:6-7).

Chapter 5
Things to Come

"Then you will be arrested, persecuted, and killed. You will be hated all over the world because you are my followers" (Matthew 24:9).

I read a news article recently that has grieved my heart. The title of the news article was "France Under Attack After Church Beheading." Three people were killed, one beheaded apparently just for believing in Jesus. It immediately reminded me of Jesus speaking in Matthew 24 about when He would return. If you are not familiar with it, I would recommend that you read all of it. I am only going to address verse 9, since that is what I thought of when I read the article.

In context, Jesus was speaking to His disciples about the future they would face because of their faith in Him. His message to them became a reality. Here is how each of the apostles died. I have included Paul as he is referred to as "the Apostle to the Gentiles."

Peter - Crucified on a cross. He requested to be crucified upside down as he felt unworthy to be crucified in the same manner as Christ.

Andrew - Crucified on a cross bound by rope instead of nails and hung upside down in the form of an X. He felt unworthy to be hung in the cross position.

James - The first to die by the sword after Christ was executed.

John - The only apostle to die of old age.

Phillip - History has not recorded how he died.

Bartholomew - Flayed and beheaded.

Thomas - Also known as *doubting* Thomas, He was stabbed to death with spears.

Matthew - Early Church Fathers believe he was stoned, burned, beaten, and beheaded.

James - Pushed from the pinnacle of the temple, then stoned and beaten to death.

Jude - All we know is that the King of Syria had him *martyred* for commanding demons to come out of idols. The method in which he was martyred is unknown.

Simon the Zealot - Was sawed in half.

Judas Iscariot - Hung himself for betraying Jesus.

Matthias – Unknown but was believed to be stoned to death.

Paul - Beheaded by Nero in 68 A.D.

There are those who would tell you that Christ death and resurrection was a hoax. Some would call it a scam, while still others would simply call the resurrection account a lie. I find it interesting that if this was a hoax that not one of these apostles spoke up to save their lives. They were there and bore witness that Jesus was who He said He was. Men will die for a worthy cause, but I do not know of any who would die for a lie.

At no time in recent history do I remember such hostility towards people for simply believing in Jesus. I do not think it is just a period that will soon pass. Over the past several years I have seen this hostility grow. Now it is to the point where many believers are afraid to even mention their faith for fear of rejection and in extreme situations, bodily harm.

Let me say at this point, that much of this is our own fault. For many years we have lifted up everything in our faith except the one thing Christ asked us to lift up - Him! Many of those *things* I sincerely believe in, but they have been communicated sometimes with anger and contempt, rather than with the love that Christ showed us when He forgave us and welcomed us into His *fold*, the True Church. Jesus addressed this in that same passage of Scripture in verse ten: *"And many will turn away from me and betray and hate each other."* We have even attacked each other simply because we attend different denominational churches, or we interpret Scripture a little differently from one another with each one believing that his or her interpretation is the correct one. I think we all may be in for a shock when Christ returns. The saying that *Christians shoot their wounded* is more than a cliché; it is sadly true.

Nevertheless, here we are 2,000 years after Christ said it would begin to happen in the end. Our friends in many parts of the world are being kidnapped and tortured as I write this. Many will have limbs brutally severed until they disavow their relationship with Christ. Others will be murdered. According to the Center for the Study of Global Christianity (CSGC), over 100,000 Christians have been murdered each year for the past 10 years! That is one million people who have been martyred for the simple reason that they believe in the Son of God. Even though I know this to be a fact, I cannot comprehend it. And don't be fooled into believing that this cannot happen in America. The hatred towards Christians abounds. There is no need for me to elaborate on the point.

It is hard to believe that in the freest nation on earth, one founded on Judeo-Christian principles, that Christians are now being persecuted for their faith. We are not being burned at the stake, but persecution comes in various forms. The definition of persecution includes hostility and ill treatment because of race or political or religious beliefs. Just ask any African American who was raised in the fifties and sixties if they were persecuted for the color of their skin and you will get a resounding "yes!" Now that same prejudice is aimed at evangelical Christians today. Jesus included vile accusations and lies about Christians in Matthew 5:11-12: *"Blessed are you when they revile and persecute you and say all kinds of evil against you falsely for My sake."*

With this understanding let me name just a few illustrations of Christian persecution that I am aware of.

Jack Phillips - A baker who has been dragged in and out of court all the way to the Supreme Court for refusing to make some of the most profane cakes. He was simply trying to run his business as a Christian businessman and was targeted for it.

Barronille Stutzman - A florist who was forced into retirement because she refused to compromise her Christian values and participate in the sinful celebration of homosexual marriage.

Joe Kennedy – A coach who was fired for exercising his first amendment rights to pray in public.

Many would call this discrimination, but make no mistake about it, this is persecution, and the worst is still to come. It is time we as Christians need to wake up and take a stand! We might not be killed and slaughtered, at least not yet, but that doesn't mean that our children or grandchildren will not be sent to prison for refusing to say that a man can become a woman.

I need to get to my purpose before you get bored and do not read the rest of this. The fact that Christ is coming back is a reality. I believe many of us need a startling *gut-check* to this fact. I think that if we really believed that His return was imminent, it would change the way we treat one another, how close we truly walk with the Lord, and our priorities would become the same as the priorities of our Lord. Verse twelve listed above pretty much sums it up as to where I believe we are in this move toward His coming: *"Sin will be rampant everywhere, and the love of many (His followers) will wax cold."* Thank God for the next verse. *"But he that endures to the end will be saved"* (v.13).

Chapter 6
God's Plan

"I know the plans I have for you says the Lord. They are plans for good and not disaster, to give you a future and a hope" (Jeremiah 29:11).

God's people found themselves in exile after Jerusalem had been taken captive by Babylon. It was in this setting that God gave the above promise to Jeremiah to give to His people. But it would be another seventy years before they would see God's promise fulfilled. Until then, they would remain as exiled slaves to the Babylonians. It must have been very difficult for the Israelites to put much faith in Jeremiah's prophecy or in God himself under those difficult circumstances. They would face hardships and tragedy during those seventy years and many who were given the promise, died before they had the chance to see that day arrive.

It is hard to see and believe that God has a plan for our future, one that brings hope, when we are in the midst of adversity. Early this evening, one of my neighbors stopped by to let me know that his brother-in-law had just died. Can you imagine what his response would be if I had told him not to worry, that God was planning an excellent future for him? When my wife lost her two sons, people really tried their best to console her. Two phrases that would reduce her to tears were, "It must have been God's will," and "It must be part of God's plan for you." The last thing a grieving mother wants to hear is that it is God's plan.

When Covid came on the scene in 2020 it brought adversity, fear, and panic throughout the entire world. Now, three years later there doesn't seem to be a good end within the foreseeable future. There are so many that have been affected by this pandemic. Many have died. Jobs have been lost, and in many parts of the world people are literally starving to death either for lack of money, or a shortage of available food. We would be hard pressed to convince anyone affected by this pandemic that this was a part of God's plan to give us a future and a hope.

Joseph was just a child when his angry brothers threw him into a pit and then sold him to a group of Midianites who took him to Egypt. He ended up in Potiphar's court only to be falsely accused of trying to rape Potiphar's wife. He landed in prison where he spent years until he was called upon by King Pharaoh to interpret a dream. Doing so, he was released from prison and became the second most powerful man in Egypt. When famine hit the land, Joseph was put in charge of distributing food throughout the entire nation. He saved millions of lives, was reunited with his father and brothers, and he was able to keep his family from starvation. Here is what he said to his brothers upon their asking forgiveness: *"you meant it for harm, but God meant it for good."* I am confident that from being thrown in a pit, to becoming a slave, to a dark dingy dungeon, Joseph often wondered, "why me Lord?" In the end Joseph could look back and see that God had orchestrated each and every step along the way in order that Joseph could save his family and an entire nation during a time of adversity.

When tragedy comes our way, we cannot see its purpose in our lives at the time. We constantly ask God why! We cannot see into the future for answers any better than Joseph could. Yet through it all the promise of God still holds true. God has a plan, a plan for good and not disaster – a plan for a brighter future, something to give us hope. Look beyond the trouble of today. Look into the future with faith and hope that God has a plan. He will bring us through the difficulties of life, whether they be a pandemic, loss of jobs, or even the loss of loved ones. There is a brighter future just around the corner - one with no tears or heartache, no sickness or pain, no more death. Place your faith in a loving God and look to the future with a hope that only God can give.

Chapter 7
Christlikeness

"Work hard to show the results of your salvation, obeying God with deep reverence and fear. For God is working in you, giving you the desire and the power to do what pleases Him" (Philippians 2: 12).

Two years ago, I challenged myself to pray daily that God would help me to do 3 things: 1) Think with the mind of Christ, 2) See with the eyes of Christ, and 3) Hear with the ears of Christ. I originally kept that prayer to myself. Then feeling the need to be held accountable, I posted it on my social media for everyone to see, so that I would be held accountable. Well, to date no one has challenged me. I am pretty sure it is not because I have accomplished my goal, since I know that I am far short of it. However, as I have been doing this, it has called into question a lot of my former theological beliefs about Christlikeness. Most of you who read this will most likely reject what I am about to say, but I can only hope that before you dismiss it totally, you will at least pray about it and think about the Scriptures I will present to make my case. Some will even believe that I am being arrogant or prideful. Nothing could be further from the truth. I have never been more humbled, and I have never felt closer to God in my seventy-two years of life than I do today. It is truly joy unspeakable and peace that passes all understanding.

So, is it possible in this life to be like Christ? Let me clarify that I am not asking if I can be perfect. That would be impossible since I was born a sinner and lived a lot of years outside the will of God. The only man who lived a sinless life from beginning to end was Jesus Christ. But what about after I surrender my life to Him; after I have asked Christ to forgive my sins, to come and live in my heart?

Is it possible to really live a holy life, one that rises above sin, one that is totally surrendered to God through the infilling of the Holy Spirit? The short answer is found in Matthew 19:26: *"But Jesus looked at them and said, with men this is impossible, but with God all things are possible."*

This makes it pretty clear that the answer is a resounding "yes!" Paul said in Galatians 2:20: *"My old self has been crucified with Christ. It is no longer I who live, but Christ lives in me. So, I live in this earthly body by trusting in the Son of God, who loved me and gave Himself for me."* To be crucified with Christ means that I have died. My old nature has not just been wounded; it has been killed. That is why Paul said it is not me who is living anymore, it is Christ that is living in my body. He *"gave himself,"* not to make it tolerable to live in this sinful world, but to be set free from it completely.

For further affirmation that we are to die to our old nature and allow Christ to live in us through a new nature, that is to say *His* nature, consider this passage:

"Since you have been raised to new life with Christ, set your sights on the realities of heaven, where Christ sits in the place of honor at God's right hand. Think about the things of heaven and not the things of earth. For you died to this life and your real life is hidden with Christ in God. And when Christ Who is your life is revealed to the whole world, you will share in all His glory. So put to death the sinful earthly things lurking within you. Put on your new nature and be renewed as you learn to know your creator and become like Him (Colossians 3:1-5).

Once I commit my life to Christ, He expects that I become obedient in following Him. When God's nature comes to replace our old nature our desire changes in the process. My desire gets replaced by His desire along with my old nature being replaced with His nature. His nature, plus His desire, equals His power unleashed within us.

We can then *"live every day as more than conquerors through Christ who loves us"* (Romans 8:37).

I was taught that once I accepted Christ as my Savior and received salvation, I didn't need to do anything more; that I was complete at that point. The writer of Hebrews said this in chapter six verse nine: *"We are persuaded better things of you, things that accompany salvation."* Those things that accompany salvation are the dying of my old nature and His nature coming to live in me. My desire dies with my old nature and His desire becomes alive within me. When this occurs, I have His power to overcome anything, and I do mean anything that life throws at me.

In 1 Thessalonians 4:7 we read these words: *"God has called us to live Holy lives, not impure lives. Therefore, anyone who refuses to live by these rules is not disobeying human teaching but is rejecting God, who gives His Holy Spirit to you."* We cannot live both impure lives and pure lives at the same time. It goes against the very nature of who God is and how He is calling us to live in this life. He has given us the Holy Spirit for the very purpose of overcoming impure living. Failure to live in the victory He has provided is rejecting God. This is not just conjecture on my part, but literally what the Scripture here is saying.

At this point you are probably having one of several reactions to what I have presented thus far. You may think I have really gone off the deep end to think that I can live a holy life here on earth. Some may even go so far as to say I am a heretic to think I can become like Christ. And just to be clear, I do not mean a reasonable likeness of Christ, but to be like Christ. Finally, I pray that a few of you are saying, *these Scriptures sound logical, and I know I could live closer to God than what I am currently.* If you fall into that category, please read on.

So how do I achieve this level of Christlikeness? You don't! He has already done it for you. When Christ breathed His last words from the Cross, He uttered these words, *"It is finished!"* Not in part, but completely. He has already done for you all that is needed for you to have that level of victory in your life. Let me start explaining how Christlikeness can happen with a passage from 1 John 2:15-17: *"Do not love the world or the things in the world. If anyone loves the world, the love of the Father is not in Him. For all that is in the world—the desires of the flesh and the desires of the eyes and the pride of life—is not from the Father but is from the world."*

I underlined the part of this passage that distinguishes our loving the world vs., the love of the Father not being in us. Let me say it another way. When the love of the Father is in us, the love for the world goes away. It is replaced by the things God loves; by the very nature of Him living within us.

There are at least two more things that God has provided to us that we may be the living image of His Son. Jesus made this commitment to us in John 14:12: *"Truly, truly, I say unto you, whoever believes in me will also do the works that I do; and greater works than these will you do, because I am going to my Father."*

My first thought when I was praying over these words from Christ himself was, *I can't even think that I could do more than Jesus did. It would be sacrilegious to even think that.* But I couldn't escape the fact that Jesus said it. How can it be that not only will I do the works that He did, but that I could do greater works? The answer lies at the end of the passage: *"Because I go to the Father".*

The second thing that Jesus has done for us is that He mediates between us and the Heavenly Father for everything on our behalf. Most people upon hearing these words of Jesus tend to associate them with the miracles He performed. It means so much more than that. I will only focus on the one thing that He did that speaks to the point I am trying to make. For forty days He wandered in the wilderness being tempted of the devil and He came out victorious. He defeated every attempt of the enemy to cause Him to sin. Hebrews 4:15 tells us this: *"For we do not have a high priest who is unable to sympathize with our weaknesses, but we have one who has been tempted in every way, just as we are, yet without sin."* By His defeating sin in His human form, He has shown us that we can as well, and He petitions the Father on our behalf every second of every day for the grace and power of the Godhead to make it so.

We have seen in Scripture thus far that when Christ was crucified on the Cross, He made it possible for our sinful nature to be crucified as well. In addition, He makes intercession on our behalf twenty-four hours a day, seven days a week for us to access all the power the heavenly Father has to give.

If that wasn't enough, He makes one third and final resource available to us to overcome the world - the Holy Spirit. Luke 24:49: *"And now I will send the Holy Spirit just as my Father promised. Stay here in the city until the Holy Spirit comes and fills you with power from heaven."*

When we allow God to fill us with His Holy Spirit there is no room for anything else to exists within us. It doesn't just fill us with some mystical spirit of some sort. It fills us with power from heaven:

Power to defeat the enemy in our lives.
Power to minister in Jesus' name.
Power to love rather than hate.
Power to forgive others who have wronged us.
Power to overcome the tragedies that happen in our lives.
Power to live victorious lives each and every day here on earth.

What more could God possibly do for us? He died to cleanse us from all sin, He makes intercession for us to God the Father, and

He has sent us the Holy Spirit that allows us to be filled with all the power in the heavens.

The only thing required of us is to truly offer up our sinful nature to be nailed to the Cross in exchange of a new nature - His nature. When we do that, all the work to be *a better Christian* ceases. It is not about our daily struggle to be better. It is about surrender. We surrender the fact that we cannot do this ourselves and we allow Him to do it for us.

Let me give a personal example. God brought two men into my life a few years ago who seemed to oppose me at everything I was attempting to accomplish in ministry. I say that God brought them into my life because He needed to teach me something that would take me deeper into my relationship with Him. I would stand my ground and defend the work God was trying to do. I likened it to Peter when he cut off the ear of the Roman soldier in defending Christ. Instead of commending Peter, Jesus rebuked Him and put the ear back on the soldier. What I learned is that God did not need me to defend Him. What He needed me to do was to love those men that He had placed in my life; to love those whom I felt were persecuting me. I offered them up to God and instantly, my anger was replaced with peace and my heart was filled with His compassion. All I had to do was to accept what God had already made available to me.

There is an old hymn we used to sing in church. It was used many times for a call to repentance. It was called *I Surrender All.* The chorus said, *I surrender all. All to Jesus I surrender. I surrender all.* Not just part of my life, but all of it; my anger, my fear, and my doubts. Then there are those areas that I want to hang on to that come from this world - my money, my job, my vices. He becomes the number one thing in my life above and beyond anything and everything else. When I surrender to that level, He does the rest, and I will have achieved Christlikeness.

Chapter 8
Thinking of Others

"Is there any encouragement from belonging to Christ? Any comfort from His love? Any fellowship together in the Spirit? Are your hearts tender and compassionate? Then make me truly happy by agreeing wholeheartedly with each other, loving one another, and working together with one mind and purpose. Don't be selfish; don't try to impress others. Be humble, thinking of others as better than yourself" (Philippians 2: 1-5).

I would like to give you the *Williams* paraphrase of this passage: *"We should be extremely encouraged because we now belong to the Savior of the world! Because we belong to Him, His Spirit lives in us and guides our thoughts and gives us direction. The result is a tender compassionate heart with love for my fellow man, so much so that I think of others more highly than I think of myself."*

This passage is often referred to as *have the attitude of Christ.* Since I have committed to praying for this very thing, it caught my attention. I was doing okay until I got to the part that says: *"Be humble and think of others more highly than yourself."* That is a hard one. Think of others more highly than myself. The writer must have known I would have a struggle with that, so he followed it up by saying, *"don't look out only for your own interest, but take an interest in others too."*

Okay, I try to do that with my family and friends. But what about those who do not share my personal beliefs? How do I show an interest in those who have a different political view? Trust me, I have some pretty strong views on politics and if I am honest, I expect others to share those views. What about race, or religion? I could go into a lot of detail, but I think you get where I am coming from. How do we show interest in others that do not share our worldviews?

I even teach about this when doing Discipleship seminars. We should adapt to other cultures instead of expecting them to adapt to ours. I think that is what Paul had in mind when he said, "*I have become all things to all people so that by all possible means I might save some*" (1 Corinthians 9:22 NIV).

Our country has entered an era where it is acceptable to believe anything, or to be anything you want, as long as you are not Christian! It is hard to think of others more highly than yourself when they are calling you a bigot for believing in the sanctity of marriage, or that boys are boys, and girls are girls. Yet, that is exactly what God expects of us. We are not to love only those who act and believe like us. We are to also love those around us who are different in their worldview.

Another Scripture comes to mind, "*While we were yet sinners, Christ died for us.*" I am often heard saying, "when Paul called himself the chief of all sinners, I had not been born yet." I know of no one who has been more undeserving of Christ's love and forgiveness than I have. Despite all the hatred and venom I demonstrated toward God and His Son, He thought enough of me to lay His life down on the Cross for me. Now He expects me to be willing to put others above myself and show them the same level of love and forgiveness as He did. The only way I know to accomplish this in my life is to see others through the eyes of the Christ. I must crucify my sinful nature on the Cross and allow God's nature to take its place.

I get frustrated listening to the different arguments about destroying national monuments. Or hearing the challenge, *is it black lives matters, or all lives matters?* Or *are Democrats evil, or is it Republicans?* On vacation, within minutes of passing through D.C., I began to see the confederate flag being flown from the back of pickup trucks and by the time I reached Tennessee you couldn't pass any retail store without the opportunity to purchase one. I wondered if those who fly them even knew the real history of that flag, or how it was changed four times before we ended up with this version, steeped in the Jim Crow era. It angered me and I found myself thinking (not saying) how stupid they must be.

Then I read this verse: *"think of others more highly than yourself and take an interest in them too."* So, here I sit, typing this for all to see. How should we apply this passage, not just to those who share our viewpoints, but to those who don't? I have purposely put myself in positions that require me to apply this principle of thinking of others more highly than myself.

It is my personal belief, after walking with the Lord for over fifty years, that you must earn the right to speak into someone's life personally before discussing their spiritual standing with God. If you are serious about soul winning, I challenge you to use Christ's example with His disciples. He spent three years with them preparing them to go out and take His place after He would ascend back to heaven. By building personal relationships, we build trust with others as well as their seeing into our personal lives, both the good and the bad.

In regard to those whom we find difficult to think of more highly than ourselves, likely they are the ones we need to build relationships with the most. Let me offer one example from my life that represents what I am trying to say. Twenty-five years ago, God placed a young man in my life. We had absolutely nothing in common. Tom was a chronic alcoholic, as well as drug addict. In those early years I never had a conversation with Tom when he wasn't either high or drunk. He would lie to me, threaten to physically harm me, and treat me with disrespect. Yet I knew that this was one of God's children and I was to put his need for Christ above my own personal feelings and beliefs. To say that it was difficult sometimes would be an understatement, but I stayed faithful to Tom and my commitment to think of him more highly than myself. Others that were part of our team would often ask me, "when are you going to give up on Tom?" I always replied, "when God gives up on me." Here we are twenty-five years later, and Tom is no longer a friend; he is family. He has sat at my table on Thanksgiving Day and at Christmas. We talk on the phone and stay in touch regularly. Before leaving my former ministry to start another one, I was being honored for my years of service with the organization. Tom spoke at that event and here is what he said, "people today have all kinds of heroes they look up to. Some look up to professional athletes, others look up to movie stars; none of which they are ever going to know or have a relationship with. Richard you are my hero. You believed in me when I did not believe in myself. No one else wanted to have anything to do with me, and honestly, I didn't like me either. But you never gave up on me. You took the abuse and the lies, and I finally realized that I could do this, I could change. Thank you, Richard, for being my friend, you will always be my hero."

Needless to say, I was reduced to tears. I am not sharing this to build myself up. I want you to see and understand what can happen if we are truly willing to think of others more highly than ourselves. It requires time and sacrifice. Sometimes it might even be questioned by others. But if you remain faithful, you can change lives and lay the fruit of souls at the feet of Jesus.

Chapter 9
My Desire Vs. His Desire/Doing the Will of God

You won't spend the rest of your lives chasing your own desires, but you will be anxious to do the Will of God" (1 Peter 4:2).

I just finished my morning devotional and prayer time. I feel compelled to share just a couple of verses this morning that came out of my time with the Lord. I encourage those who seek to follow Christ to read the whole chapter of I Peter chapter 4. Really ponder how it applies to your life today. There are two verses that spoke to me in my devotion, the first is 1 Peter 4: 2; the second passage is 1 Peter 4:7-8. I will speak to that passage in a moment.

Much of my life was spent chasing my own desires while at the same time wanting to know that I was *doing* what God would have me to do. Many times, my chasing after *things* came before my desire to *do His will*. I wouldn't admit it, or maybe couldn't, but if I am brutally honest, it is true. How much more could I have accomplished if I had put His will before that of satisfying my own desires. I could make a very long list of what those desires were that came before my desire for God, but I sense that it isn't necessary. Most likely as you are reading this you are taking inventory of your own life to see if your desires are the same as His. I will ask this question of you just as I had to ask it of myself. "How much of your income is spent on the things of God vs. the things you want for yourself - the houses, the cars, and the personal *toys* we like to have?" Compare that to those who are homeless, or addicted. How much is spent to make the world a better and safer place? Compare the two and see where the balance scale tilts. Do the same thing with your time. How much of it is spent with the Lord, praying, reading your Bible, and worshiping Him vs. social media, or television? When we totally surrender to God, there is a change that takes place within our heart and mind. The desires change. Instead of our personal desires, the desires of God take their place. If that has not happened in your life, I highly recommend that you talk with the Lord about it.

This leads me to the second Scriptures that spoke to me. Verses 7 and 8: *"The end of the world is coming soon, be earnest and disciplined in your prayers. Most important of all, continue to show deep love for each other, for love covers a multitude of sins."* This is the only answer for our broken and fallen world today. When we totally surrender our desires to God, He replaces them with His desires. One of those desires is that no one should perish. The only way there could ever be any chance of that happening would be to declare war on sin. The Bible also says in 2 Chronicles 7:14: *"If my people who are called by my name would humble themselves and pray and seek my face and turn from their wicked ways, I will hear from Heaven, I will forgive their sins and I will heal their land."*

It doesn't say to just love those I like, or who share my personal values. It simply says show *deep* love for each other. I remembered back when the Amish children were so brutally murdered in their classroom. If ever there was a reason for those Amish families to harbor anger and hatred that would have been it. Instead, they embraced the family of the shooter, even to the point of sharing the monetary donations that came flooding in.

What would our world look like if we followed that example; whites really showing *deep* love for blacks, blacks showing *deep* love to the police, and the police showing *deep* love to those whom they have been chosen to protect? I could list a long litany of ways this would apply, but hopefully you get the point I am trying to make. As for the praying part, I promise if you master the love part, prayer will come easily.

So, for everyone who claims to be Christian, I challenge you to read this entire chapter of 1Peter 4. Ask yourself and ask God what He would ask of you as you seek to live a life here on earth that would be pleasing to Him. I am doing the same.

Chapter 10
Prayer

"We ask God to give you complete knowledge of His will and to give you spiritual wisdom and understanding. Then the way you live will always honor and please the Lord and your lives will produce every kind of good fruit. All the while you will grow as you learn to know God better and better" (Colossians 1:9-10).

There is more to the prayer in verses eleven and twelve. But start with this. Make it a personal request to God just for you. Consistently and often. Don't be surprised *when* you hear back from Him.

A very dear friend recently asked me a question on how to pray to God. It's a question that I have been asked before. I gave a very quick response something like, "you just talk to him like you are having a conversation." I have been thinking about that question and my answer frequently since that day. I've just started studying prayer in the Bible as a result. I've discovered that the words pray, prayer, and prayed are found 375 times in Scripture. Within those Scriptures I have also discovered two other important truths. 1) Prayer is the catalyst that makes things happen in our lives, our family, and even the world. 2) It is a two-way street.

I have been blessed to serve the Lord for fifty years now. I wish that I could say that I never disappointed God in my walk, but that would be a lie. During those fifty years I have failed Him many times through the circumstances of my life. The one thing I feel that I have gotten right is understanding the importance of prayer in the life of a believer. In my study on prayer, I tried to find and read every prayer in the Bible. I discovered that every prayer I read that was being prayed directly to God from a point of intimacy, or burdened heart,

God joined the conversation. What?! You are now asking; do you mean God actually spoke back? Yes, that is exactly what I am saying. Whether it was an audible voice, or a prompting of the Spirit I don't know. But does that really matter? The point is, God joined the conversation. The problem of *hearing* God is on our end, not His. First, if we are honest, very few develop a consistent prayer life at all. We seldom pray and if we do, it is very short with a list of our needs. If I rarely spoke to my wife, and then when I did only ask her to do things for me, I sense that intimacy would pretty much fly out the window.

Why did God put so much emphasis on prayer? Why was it so important to Him? The answer is quite simple and straight forward; God longs to have an intimate relationship with all of us. That was His intent of creating mankind. When having that kind of relationship with Him becomes important to us, I can promise you *He will* join the conversation. It is just a matter of us learning how to really pray. It is not about the *thee's* and *thou's, and oh God's,* and the moans and groans. It is simply having a conversation with Him.

I have read over a hundred verses in the Bible that deals with prayer. Time and space will not allow me to speak to each of them. I will look at several here now, but if you truly want to know how to pray, what to pray for, and how God answers our prayers, I encourage you to read them all.

Philippians 4:6 gives us a glimpse of how we should approach prayer and what to pray for: *"Don't be anxious about anything, but in everything by prayer and supplication, with thanksgiving let your request be known to God."*

- Don't be anxious, for we do not have to fear to ask, or worry whether God will hear our prayers.
- Supplication… be humble.

- Be thankful.
- Make requests.

Matthew 6:6: *"When you pray, go into your room, close the door, and pray to your Father, who is unseen. And your Father, who sees in secret, will reward you"* (NIV). We need those times in our lives when we just spend time with God alone. It is during these types of prayer that I usually hear from Lord.

Jeremiah 33:3: *"Call to me and I will answer you, and I will tell you great and hidden things that you have not known."* God's promise to Jeremiah was that if He prayed God promised to answer Him. God is always waiting to hear from us. Any time we call (pray) God's promise is that He will always, not most of the time, but always answer us. Do you ever wonder what God is thinking? Do you wonder what He has in store for you? Do you wonder if God is happy with where you are in life spiritually? Well, here is His promise to answer you and to reveal great things and things you have never thought about.

Colossians 4:2: *"Continue steadfastly in prayer, being watchful in it with Thanksgiving."* In 1 Thessalonians 5:16-17, Paul phrases it a little differently by saying, *"Pray without ceasing."* Paul is challenging us to have an ongoing consistent prayer life where we are always able to both talk to God and hear from Him. If we are steadfast (consistent) in our prayer time, if we consistently pray, this is when our thoughts become His thoughts and our actions reflect the actions God would take by the mere fact of His living within us. This is enough in itself to be thankful to God for wanting that kind of intimacy with all who call themselves by His name.

Matthew 26:41: *"Watch and pray that you may not fall into temptation, The spirit indeed is willing, but the flesh is weak."* A man had two dogs. One was a large vicious dog that wanted to kill the other dog. Every day the owner had to watch over the weaker dog for fear of it being maimed or killed by the much bigger dog. Finally, the owner began feeding the weaker dog and ignoring the bad one. The smaller dog began to grow and gain strength day by day while the vicious dog grew weaker by the day. In the end the smaller dog became so strong that he could defeat the one that desired to destroy him. Our enemy, the devil, seeks to devour us each and every day. We need that extra strength so that our spirit becomes stronger than our flesh. The way God provides that extra nourishment to our spirit is through constant contact with Him through prayer. Satan cannot eat from the table of the Master. That *spiritual food* is only available to you and me. We access it through prayer.

Matthew 6:9-13: *"Pray then like this: 'Our Father in Heaven hallowed be Your name. Your kingdom come, your will be done, on earth as it is in heaven. Give us this day our daily bread and forgive us our debts as we forgive the debtors. And lead us not into temptation but deliver us from evil.'"*

- Approach God with a humble and respectful heart.
- Pray that His will, will be done in you, and the world around you, now and not just when you get to heaven.
- Pray for your needs to be met. I'm not just referring to your physical needs but especially your spiritual needs.
- Far too many Christians spend little or no time asking God for strength to overcome the temptations in their lives resulting in spiritual defeat within us.
  Also study these references: Philippians 4:6, Mark 11:24, Roman 8:26, James 5:16, 1 Thessalonians 5:16-18.

God would be more than pleased if after we pray, we ask Him what He would have to say to us each day. Some questions you could say to invite God into the conversation could be like this:

- Lord, what is on your heart today?
- What is it you want in my life today?
- How can I serve you today, Father?

Then just sit for a while and listen. He promised that if you would call out to Him, He would answer you and reveal the hidden things of Himself.

Chapter 11
Complete Harmony

"We who are strong must be considerate of those who are sensitive (weak) about things like this. We should not please ourselves. We should help others do what is right and build them up in the Lord. For even Christ didn't live to please Himself. As the Scriptures say, 'The insults of those who insult You, oh God, have fallen on me.' Such things were written in the Scriptures long ago to teach us. And the Scriptures gives us hope and encouragement as we wait patiently for God's promises to be fulfilled. May God, who gives this patience and encouragement help you live in complete harmony with each other as is fitting for followers of Christ Jesus. Therefore, accept each other just as Christ has accepted you so that God will be given the glory" (Romans 15:1-7).

In Romans 14, Paul had been addressing those who he called *weak* in the faith. He identifies those who must measure their spirituality by the things they do, or don't do; things such as not eating certain types of meat, or drinking certain things, or even what day of the week they worship.

Paul continues that theme in Romans 15:1. He refers to those who must follow a set of rules as weaker brothers and sisters. It would be the weaker believer who would criticize a woman for wearing too much makeup or wearing pants to church. This was causing strife and discord between what Paul referred to as weaker believers and the stronger ones in faith who needed no help in their spiritual walk with the Lord.

I have witnessed this type of arguing in the Church for fifty-eight years as a believer. *Did you see that dress that sister Mary was wearing in church? Well, I saw deacon Jones with a beer in his hand the other day! Jane had way too much makeup on, it makes her look like Jezebel!* To me it is fitting that the Bible refers to these people as the weaker of believers. It must break the heart of God to see how off the beaten path we have become that so many measure their spirituality by such things as church attendance, or what we wear to church. Others measure their faith by how much they give to the church. But the worst form of what I deem as legalism occurs when I measure my spirituality by putting someone else down.

Rather than tearing one another apart over these matters, we should be living in complete harmony with our fellow believers. The world is watching how we treat one another. Listen to Jesus' words in His last prayer just before being crucified. *"I have given them the glory that you gave me, so they may be one, as we are one. I am in them, and you are in me. May they experience such perfect unity that the world will know that you sent me and that you love them as much as you love me"* (John 17: 22-23).

This is the only answer for our broken and fallen world today. The Bible makes it clear that we as believers are not to judge others. But this passage makes it just as clear that God has given the rest of the world the right to judge us according to how we treat others. It doesn't say to just love those who share my theological understanding of Scripture, or who share my personal values. It simply says to love one another and if we do this one simple thing, the world will know we are his disciples.

So, for everyone who claims to be Christian, I challenge you to take Christ's prayer seriously. Ask yourself, and ask God how He would have you to love others. If you truly seek to live a life here on earth that would be pleasing to Him, you cannot get there without responding to His prayer to love one another.

Is there anyone who does not see a need for healing our land? We should be offering hope and encouragement rather than judgement and condemnation. Be patient with the immature believers, offering them hope from a loving God. Instead of judging one another, we should find ways to bring about what we would call complete harmony.

To me the message is clear: we need each other! Life isn't just about me. When God approached Cain and asked where Abel was, Cain asked God this question, "Am I my brother's keeper?" In short, the Bible teaches us that yes, indeed, I am my brother's keeper. If you are reading this, I want you to know that during my *weak times*" you are what gives me the strength to carry on. In turn, as we walk through those weak times it allows me the ability to empathize with you and to walk through your valleys when they arise. We can give each other hope and excitement to know that *all* of God's promises will one day be fulfilled for all of us. I thank God for all of you that God has placed in my life. May we always be there for each other in the ups and downs life will give us until God's promises come to pass for us all.

Chapter 12
Doubt

"The father cried out, 'I do believe, but help me overcome my unbelief.'" (Mark 9:24).

This father had enough faith that he brought his demon possessed son to Jesus for healing. Yet within himself the father must have had reservations as to whether Jesus really could heal his son. When asking Jesus to heal his son, he ended his request with "if you can." Jesus snaps back at the father with, "what do you mean, 'if I can?'" We often do a version of that ourselves when we pray "if it is your will." Adding that little phrase to the end of our prayers gives us an out if our prayers are not answered as we would have them answered. Have you ever prayed for someone's healing and added that phrase at the end of your healing prayer? Maybe you were praying for a new job, and you added that phrase "if it would be your will." That always gives us the ultimate excuse if we do not see the results we prayed for.

If we are honest with ourselves, doubt is something that all of us struggle with from time to time. The question arises, is it ok to have doubt in our walk with God? After all, isn't the definition of doubt the absence of faith? Here a father has come to seek the One he has heard so much about. He has heard of the miracles Jesus had performed, and perhaps he had actually witnessed some of them. Now his son needs a miracle, and he is asking the Lord to heal his son. Jesus asks him, "do you believe?" His immediate answer, "Yes, but help me with my unbelief." He believed enough to seek Jesus out because he knew Jesus could heal his son, but doubt was creeping in. Perhaps he was thinking, I know He can do it, but maybe He won't do it for me.

There were others in the Bible who expressed doubt. John the Baptist is just one of many examples in Scripture of very faithful followers who at one time or another expressed their doubt. This is the man who proclaimed the coming of Christ and when he saw Jesus coming toward the river to be baptized, John proclaimed Him as the Savior even before Jesus ever spoke a word. John heard the voice of God declare Jesus as His Son and witnessed the dove which came down to rest on Jesus' shoulder. Fast forward and we find John locked up in prison, no doubt justifiably in fear for his life. He sends one of his followers to ask Jesus this question, "are you the Messiah, or do we need to look for someone else?" His faith was strong until he was faced with extreme adversity. Then he had doubt. Peter doubted once he got out of a boat to go to Jesus and began to sink. Thomas had doubt that Jesus had even been resurrected.

I have been asked several times in my life if it is okay to have doubt. There are certainly those preachers who would tell you *no*. In fact, I have heard some of them express it as sin against God. But I am not so sure. Here is what I do know. Jesus understood the fact that these men had doubt. Instead of condemning them He invited Thomas to touch the scars on His hands and side. When Peter began to sink, Jesus stretched out and gave Him a hand. And as for the man seeking healing for his son, instead of scolding him for his unbelief, Jesus healed his son.

I have walked with the Lord for fifty years. I have had Him to answer some pretty big prayers during those years. Time and space on Facebook prohibit me from going into detail. I would be more than happy to share either by phone or private messenger if anyone asks. During those fifty years of walking with Christ, I have become an ardent student of His Word and been the recipient of multiple miracles and answers to seemingly impossible prayer request. Yet, there are times when I have to say, *"Lord, I believe, help me with my* unbelief." Out of His mercy and grace, He always responds in the same manner as He did for Peter. He gives us an outstretched hand whenever we begin to sink into the arena of doubt.

How do we overcome doubt in our lives? Let me offer these Scriptures to help you understand how to defeat doubt.

Hebrews 12:2: *"We do this by keeping our eyes on Jesus, the champion who initiates and perfects our faith."* It wasn't until Peter took his eyes off Christ that he began to sink. Whenever we get so concerned about what is happening in our lives fear sets in, anxiety consumes us, and we begin to sink in defeat. By keeping our eyes on Jesus, we see the world through His eyes instead of through the lens of adversity.

Isaiah 41:10: *"Don't be discouraged for I am your God; I will strengthen you and help you. I will hold you up with My victorious right hand."* This is the outstretched hand of God that saved Peter from drowning. The outstretched hand of God is always there to pull you from the clutches of doubt and despair.

So, if you find yourself having doubt don't beat yourself up about it or try to hide it for fear of what someone would say. Instead, just tell the Lord your struggle. I have *no doubt* that He will be there for you.

Chapter 13
Knowing God

"For I know that my Redeemer lives, and He shall stand at last on earth; and after my skin is destroyed, this I know, that in my flesh I shall see God" (Job 19:25-26 NKJV).

Recently I was having a conversation with a dear friend where we were discussing knowing God. He stated that He wished He knew God so intimately that He never had doubts in his faith walk. I responded with something like "that would be nice." After I left, the thought of knowing God just wouldn't leave me. Is it really possible to know God to the point of having so much faith that I never doubt?

As I began to pray as well as read Scripture, I suddenly realized that the whole purpose of creation was so that God could have a relationship with mankind, one in which we come to know Him personally and intimately. For those who have just prayed a prayer of repentance and your journey has stopped there, you have missed the heart of salvation. God has so much more for us than just the forgiveness of sin. He offers Himself so that we can know everything about Him. So much so that we begin to think and act just like Him. Knowing God means more than a head knowledge of who He is. The context of Scripture means we know Him personally and intimately much like a husband knows his wife. John, in his gospel links knowing God to our salvation. *"Now this is eternal life: that they know you, the only true God, and Jesus Christ, whom you have sent"* (John 17:3).

John also penned these words at the beginning of his epistle: *"In the beginning was the Word, and the Word was with God, and the Word was God, and the Word became flesh"* (John 1:1). It is safe to say that since the

Word (Bible) is God himself, it is also safe to assume that His purpose in writing it was so that we could know Him at a very deep level. Not only will we better know God personally by reading the Bible, but we also establish a personal relationship with the holiness of God. We discover the highest level of love that God has for us, and that we can walk in that love in such a way that others will see God in us. Knowing God intimately is what led John to write these words in 1 John 3:6: *"No one who lives in Him keeps on sinning. No one who continues to sin has either seen Him or known Him."* WOW! You are having one of two reactions to this passage: either you reject it and say it is impossible, or you embrace it and seek to know God in such a way that you are driven to make it real in your life. To reject it means we reject *"The Word"* which is God. In essence I am rejecting God.

Let's look again at Paul's words about knowing Christ: *"I want to know Christ. Yes, to know the power of His resurrection and participate in His sufferings, becoming like Him in His death"* (Philippians 3:10). I can know God so deeply that I can not only understand the power of His resurrection, but I can also receive it. I know and love my wife and children so much that I would not think twice about laying my life down for them. That is what Paul is saying when he talks about sharing in the suffering of Christ. I am willing to suffer anything for the opportunity to know Christ intimately. To become just like Christ.

Prior to my accepting the call to Cityteam, I had suffered some debilitating health issues. I claimed the following verse during that time which I read regularly: *"For this reason I suffer these things, nevertheless I am not ashamed, for I KNOW whom I have believed in and am persuaded that He is able to keep that which I have committed to Him until that day"* (2 Timothy 1:12 NKJV). *That day* means His return. It is clear in this passage that knowing Him was connected to Paul's faith and the more faith I have the more knowing God becomes reality. There is another passage that I confess I have struggled to understand fully. In Romans 12:3 Paul said: *"God has dealt to each one of us a measure of faith."* My question was always, why does God give faith in measures? Did that mean that some had more measures than others? How did one determine what their measure of faith was? How would I know if I had the full measures that God intended for me?

It is clear to me now that the 2 Timothy passage was only a part of Paul's faith walk and in the Romans passage, we have a fuller picture of what it meant to him. For Paul, knowing God was directly connected to his faith in God. The more I get to know God for who He really is, the more faith He measures out to me. The more faith He measures to me, the more I can know Him. Whether or not we can ever fully know Him in this life I don't know. Our mind is finite while His is infinite. But one thing I now realize, we are to strive to know Him in that fullness every day. Today God placed this verse in front of me: *"For I KNOW that my Redeemer lives, and He shall stand at last on earth; And after my skin is destroyed, this I KNOW, that in my flesh I shall see God"* (Job 19:25-26 NKJV).

Chapter 14
The Power of Sufficient Grace

"But He said to me, 'My grace is sufficient for you, for my power is made perfect in weakness'" (2 Corinthians 12: 9-10).

This is a familiar passage of Scripture to almost everyone who follows the Christian faith. We quote it often, especially when we are having difficulties of any kind. Whenever all else fails, many Christians will quote the first part of this Scripture out of desperation. Yet for many, it still leaves them wondering why their situation doesn't change, or that God hasn't answered their prayers. Hopefully we can come to some better understanding of this passage and how it applies to our lives by the time we finish this chapter.

I was taught early on that God's grace was associated with my salvation. The theological definition being *God's undeserved favor toward man"* is usually accompanied with a Scripture such as this one found in Romans 5:8: *"And while we were yet sinners Christ died for us."* While this definition is true, it is only the beginning of what God's grace is intended to do in the life of the believer. You cannot just read the first part of this passage and stop there. You must read it in context of the whole statement. It is the second part of that Scripture that makes the *sufficient* part true. God said, *"My power is made perfect in weakness."*

God's grace equals God's power to live victorious lives here on earth. His grace is far more than just the forgiveness of our sins. It is the very essence of the believer's life. Everything I do is directly related to His grace. Even the next breath I take is because God's favor of grace allows me to take it.

Hebrews 4:15-16 helps to further understand the importance of living in grace: *"For we do not have a High Priest who is unable to sympathize with our weaknesses, but one who in every respect has been tempted as we are, yet without sin. Let us then with confidence draw near to the throne of grace, that we may receive mercy and find grace to help in time of need."*

Notice that Paul said to draw near to the throne of grace. He did not use the term near the throne of God in this instance. That is because the foundational basis for everything God does in relationship with us is based on His grace that He bestows upon us. When we realize this, we can fully understand God's undeserved favor toward man. This favor of grace reaches into every aspect of our lives.

It is in this context that grace becomes sufficient for everything we do. Not only is it sufficient to help us manage the difficulties that come in life, but in every aspect of life.

"I am certain that God who began a good work in you will continue His good work until it is finally finished on the day when Christ Jesus returns" (Philippians 1:6).

Here we have the promise that God is continually working in us to bring about perfection in our lives in preparation for the time when we will meet Christ. It is nothing that we do but rather God through the Holy Spirit is working to complete the work of grace that began when we gave ourselves to follow Him. It is His grace working within us that gives us the power to accomplish whatever God expects of us.

"Take delight in the Lord and He will give you your heart's desire" (Psalm 37:4). This passage has been misunderstood and misused by well-meaning people as well as those who do not mean so well. It has been used as a *name it and claim it* verse by those hoping to line their own pockets by saying if we are in God's favor, He will give us the

temporal desires of our heart. If we want a new car, or to become rich, all we must do is delight in the Lord and He will give us those things. This in no way is what Paul is wanting to communicate to us. When we are seriously hungry (delighted) for the things of God, He changes our desires from the temporal things of this world and replaces (gives) us spiritual desires. The act of giving us deeply spiritual desires is another act of God's grace.

To further elaborate on this let's look at Ezekiel 36:26: *"And I will give you a new heart, and I will put a new spirit in you. I will take out your stony, stubborn heart and give you a tender, responsive heart. And I will put my Spirit in you so that you will follow my decrees (desires) and be careful to obey me."*

God actually replaces our heart with a heart like His, one that is tender and responsive to the things that matter to Him. Ezekiel uses the word *responsiv*e here. In other words, we act, we carry out those desires of our new heart. It should be further noted that God did not say He would put just any new spirit in us, but that He would actually put His Spirit in us. This is the ultimate of being given the desires of His heart.

Keep in mind, as we have considered these Scriptures, the definition of grace: *God's undeserved favor to man.* We certainly have done nothing to deserve God's bestowing His own Spirit to live within us. If we can't see that as the ultimate example of God's grace, then I do not know what I could say to make the case any better.

The desires that God gives us are the desires of His heart. Another way to say it would be, we desire to do the Will of God. Hosea 6:6 gives us a glimpse of a foundational desire of His heart: *"I want you to show love not offer sacrifices. I want you to know me more than I want burnt offerings."*

What would you think is the most important desire in the heart of God; that desire that is so strong within God's heart that it rises above all His other desires? It is found in the most familiar passage of Scripture in the entire Bible, John3:16: *"For God loved us so much that He sent His Son to die for us, that if we would just believe and receive Him, that we would live with Him forever"* (William's translation).

God wants to extend His grace to us that much. It is readily available to us not only to sustain us during difficult times, or to give us salvation, but to live victorious lives through the indwelling of His Spirit. Just one more validation of God's favor to all who will receive it and walk in it.

To quote C.S. Lewis, "God calls those who receive His grace to love Him supremely and enthrone Him as their hearts desire. As they seek to do so, a paradoxical change occurs. The initial thirst of their hearts is satisfied by His grace and love. In time, this very satisfaction fuels thirst for deeper intimacy and communion with Him."

Chapter 15
The Wilderness Experience

It is difficult to capture what it is really like to have a wilderness experience by reading about it. It is just too sanitized. The feelings of the experience are missing. The sounds of the animals, the denseness of the woods surrounding you, the realization that you are alone, very alone, and that your survival in the wilderness will require your attention in detail to every move you make. One wrong move can mean you become lost in that wilderness. It has even become fatal for many a hunter who would consider themselves far from a novice.

When I was younger, I used to love to hunt and fish. Although I could never say that I was a master hunter, I feel as though I had achieved the basic skills necessary to have a decent level of success at the sport, that is until I almost became one of those hunters who failed to pay attention to the details and lost my bearings. I became lost in the wilderness!

Now that we have established that the *wilderness* is not just a leisurely walk in the woods, let's take a look at Jesus wilderness experience. I think one of the most difficult parts of a wilderness experience is that we usually do not know when or how it will end. I have often wondered if Christ knew ahead of time how many days He would be wandering; how many days would He be denied food to eat, or how many times Satan would appear to entice (tempt) Him to surrender? We cannot comprehend what it is like to be without food and water for forty days. It is difficult for me to get through more than a few hours without eating. I would be delusional after forty hours, much less forty days. That is the state of mind I believe we see in Jesus when He looks at a pile of stones and realizes He could easily turn stone into bread. When He looked down over the cities below realizing that it could all be His, He had to be wondering, when is this going to end. Even in a situation where we face the finality of life on earth, there are those moments of, when will it end? why me? and even for the strongest of believers, what is it really like when my time comes?

Do you remember what Jesus said to His mother at the wedding feast when He was asked to change the water into wine? *"My time has not yet come."* Now listen to what He says to the religious leaders after coming out of the wilderness: *"Then Jesus returned to Galilee filled with the Holy Spirit's POWER. ...He went as usual to the Synagogue on the Sabbath and stood up to read the Scriptures. The scroll of Isaiah the prophet was handed to Him. He unrolled the scroll and found the place where this was written, 'The Spirit of the Lord is upon me, for He has anointed me to bring Good News to the poor, He has sent me to proclaim that the captives will be released, that the blind will see, that the oppressed will be set free, and that the time of the Lord's favor has come'"* (Luke 4:14-19). What a contrast from the remarks to His mother. Only by entering the wilderness and defeating it could He become confident in His ability to fulfill His ministry here on earth. He was driven into the wilderness by the Holy Spirit, but once he defeated the wilderness, He possessed the Spirit's *power*!

A spiritual wilderness was not unique just to Jesus. Some of the most well-known men in the Bible experienced them. There was Elijah in 1 Kings 9, Paul in the Book of Galatians, and most significant was the nation of Israel that wandered for forty years in the wilderness before entering the Promised Land.

A spiritual wilderness experience can come in a variety of ways. It may feel like a separation from God. You might be feeling spiritually empty and have a lost interest for the things of God like prayer or reading the Bible. In an extreme case you may be like Job who suffered a devastating loss of loved ones, loss of finances, as well as his personal health.

Sometimes a spiritual wilderness is brought on simply because of the broken world we live in. However, there are times when God allows us to go through the wilderness as He did with the nation of Israel. In Deuteronomy 8:1-3, he listed four reasons why He sent them into the wilderness, reasons that are always applicable when we are in the wilderness today:

- To humble us
- To test us
- To prove our character
- To find out if we will obey His commands.

I encourage you to embrace the wilderness when you go through it, realizing that God is positioning you for what is coming next, something that will require the *power* of the Holy Spirit.

Chapter 16
The Uncertainty in Life

"Trust in the Lord with all your heart and lean not on your own understanding; in all your ways submit to Him, and He will make your paths straight" (Proverbs 3: 5-6).

If you are facing uncertainty in your life, worried about your future, or not sure what decision to make regarding a life event that has serious implications, you are not alone. One of the great examples, if not the greatest, was a decision with extremely serious implications. Abraham was directed of God to offer his son Isaac as a sacrifice to God. Would Abraham be obedient to God and sacrifice his son, or would he find a way to justify not offering Isaac up? Once everything else had been prepared for the sacrifice Isaac looks at his father and asks, *"Father, the altar is prepared but where is the sacrifice?"* Abraham's answer provides us with a glimpse into understanding Philippians 4:19 (KJV): *"But my God shall supply all your needs according to His riches in glory by Christ Jesus."* Abraham simply says to Isaac, *"God will provide."* No matter how serious or how bleak our circumstances may be, when uncertainty presents itself into our lives, God will always provide.

I had only been out of the Marine Corp a short while; I was married with two small children and my job as a wholesale grocery salesman was barely paying the bills. It was 4 am, still very dark and I was driving some seventy miles to my first meeting of the day. Suddenly, I heard someone talking to me. Yet I was alone in my car. After checking the radio to make sure it wasn't on, I dismissed it and continued my journey. Then, there it was again, "Quit your job and move to Colorado to prepare for the ministry." Anyone who knows me even casually will tell you that I am not very charismatic in my walk with the Lord. Having been raised in an era where there was a lot of abuse, and quite honestly fake charismatic doctrine, this is an area where I really *examine* the spirit before just buying in to what I am being told. I say that so you will understand the significance of what I was experiencing that morning. When I realized that I was actually hearing an audible voice of God, I pulled over on the shoulder of the road and began shaking and crying. I spent the next several minutes trying to convince myself that I wasn't crazy or hearing voices. I actually tried to have more conversation with the Lord to get Him to speak again just to validate what I thought I had heard. Nothing. Not another word audibly from that moment until this day. I have shared this experience with very few people from that day until now. However, I know that on that day, I was so in tune with God that He was a passenger in my car having a normal conversation. Whether I will ever have that experience again I don't know, but I can honestly say it has been one of the most cherished moments in my walk with the Lord.

That experience coupled with the events of the next few years of my life completely changed my relationship with God. My faith took a giant leap during those formative years in my Christian walk. There is an old Gospel song that I used to sing a lot during those early years of my walk with the Lord. I began to sing it again years later as I battled cancer. Here are the lyrics to just the first verse of that song.

Prayer is the key to Heaven
But faith unlocks the door
Words are so easily spoken
A prayer without faith
Is like a boat without an oar.

Have faith when you speak to the Master
That's all He asks you for,

Yes, prayer is the key to Heaven
But faith unlocks the door.

I speak more about the importance of faith in another chapter entitled *Walking by Faith*. The role faith plays in the life of the believer is so vital that entire books have been written about the subject and still most people only have a vague understanding how it works. I use a simple equation that explains it. Obedience + trust = faith. There is that awful word *obedience* again. The moment I mention the word there are those that will shout "legalism" or perhaps "works." I get challenged often in my disciple-making seminars when I make the statement that a disciple obediently follows the Rabbi.

This takes me back to Abraham and his sacrifice of his son Isaac. God knew in advance how Abraham would respond. He knew that Abraham would be obedient to whatever God would ask of him. That begs the question, why then did God ask this of him? It is my belief that it was for you and me. God told Abraham to do it, he obeys, trusting that God would provide, and God came through. Imagine the faith that Abraham left that mountain with by being obedient and trusting God. Repeatedly in the New Testament we see Jesus giving a command to those seeking a miracle in their lives. To the man at the pool the command was *"pick up your mat and walk;"* to Lazarus family it was *"remove the stone;"* and even something as trivial as turning the water into wine, the command was *"fill the pots with water."* Faith can never be obtained without the willingness to *trust and obey*. Hebrews chapter eleven is known as the faith chapter of the Bible. Hebrews 11:6 is the key verse, not only to the chapter, but I believe to the entire New Testament: *"And it is impossible to please God without faith. Anyone who wants to come to Him must believe that God exists and that He rewards those who diligently seek Him"*

Chapter 17
The Call

"Who has saved us and called us with a holy calling, not according to our works, but according to His own purpose and grace which was given to us in Christ Jesus before time began, but now has been revealed by the appearing of our Savior Jesus Christ, who has abolished death and brought life and immortality to light through the Gospel, to which I was appointed an apostle, and a teacher of the Gentiles" (2 Timothy 1:9 NKJV).

It was the summer of 1966 and we had just moved from my small tightknit community where I was born and raised for the first fifteen years of my life. My Father's health was declining, and his doctor had highly recommended the move because of all the pesticides used by the farmers in our area. They used crop dusters to apply the various chemicals and the chemicals would drift from the fields over the houses and settle there. The worst was when they would spray for mosquitos. It made the air thick and difficult to breath, not to mention the strong odor it created.

It was a long boring summer in my new town. I did not know anyone. School had not started, and I had not made any new friends. Then I got a phone call from a friend from back home inviting me to church camp with her youth group. I jumped at the chance, knowing I would be with my old friends that I had grown up with. I wasn't *into* church and knew very little about God, His son Jesus, or even for my need of a Savior for that matter. All I knew was that it was a chance for me to escape the boredom of my new life, and I would get to see Susie, the object of a pretty serious crush. Little did I know that this week was about to change my life and set a direction that ultimately led me to where I am today. That was fifty-five years ago and as I look back, I can see where God was always two steps ahead of me, leading me to where He wanted me to be.

On the very last night of camp something happened to me. How it began I really do not remember. It was as if I was unconscious for a few moments. I recall some teenage kid with a guitar trying to do an Elvis rendition of *Peace in the Valley*. I remember thinking how he must have wasted his money on singing lessons. He was so off-key it was all I could do to keep from laughing. That's when things went dark. The next thing I remembered was kneeling at an altar crying uncontrollably with Susie and a couple of other kids beside me. The service was over, the preacher and all the staff had left, and it was just us. I remember that Susie and the others were worried about me because I could not stop crying. Eventually, even they left, and I was all alone. Well almost alone. Something was stirring inside of me. Something I had never experienced before, and I did not know if I should embrace it or get my camp counselor to take me to the nearest mental hospital. I did not know how to describe it, nor did I know what it meant at the time, except I had this strong sense that God was staking a claim on my heart. Even then I knew that He would be calling the shots from that night on. I now know that this is what the Christian world refers to as *God's calling into full-time ministry*.

It would be twenty-five years later before I understood what the *calling of God* really was according to Scripture. In the meantime, I tried to answer *the call* as best I could from what I was taught by others who were in full-time ministry. That would mean that I was most likely called to preach, or perhaps become a foreign missionary. I settled on preaching. I will spare you the details here of that next twenty-five years' journey in learning what it really meant to be *called* of God. It ultimately led me to getting a Bible College education and settling in on becoming a pastor. I had finally found my calling, or so I thought. After all, I really enjoyed it, at least for the most part. I loved to preach sermons, and I loved shepherding those in the church. This must be it because not only was I good at it, but I also loved it!

Years passed and life happened. Finances were dangerously low; I had to take a secular job to supplement income. Finally, a debilitating illness took me out of the ministry all together. It took over a year to recover and I was anxious to return to my calling of being a full-time pastor. But there was one problem, no doors would open for me to re-enter what I had come to love so dearly and was convinced it was God's call upon my life. I was in one of the many deserts of my life that I would have to walk through. I began to doubt myself and to think that God must be punishing me for a lot of past sins in my life. Then, almost a year after my recovery, I received a phone call from someone in California wanting me to move to Pennsylvania and help start an inner-city ministry to the homeless and drug addicts. I had never seen a homeless person at the time, and I knew absolutely nothing about drug addiction. But with no job and God seemingly punishing me for something, I agreed to give it a try. God blessed the efforts, brought the right kind of people across my path, and eventually we had founded what would become a very successful ministry. Yet, it was always in the back of my mind that this southern Gospel preacher had been exiled to a strange land as punishment for the great sins of my past.

Then one day as I was taking a group tour of our mission's headquarters facilities in California, our group paused at the back of the chapel to hear the speaker talking to the residents. We were only there for a few minutes before continuing the tour. But we were there just long enough to hear him quote the Scripture found at the beginning of this chapter: *"We are called not according to our works, but according to His good will and purpose."* God used those few minutes at the back of that chapel to open my eyes and give me the true and Biblical definition of *calling.*

I wrestled with those words for some time. God, what do you mean I am not called according to my work? You called me to be a pastor, a preacher. His answer was, "No, son, I don't call anyone to be a pastor, or a missionary, or any other thing that people consider to be ministry callings. Those are the works that you do, but that is not *the call*. Your calling is to me, to be used by me for whatever purpose I need to accomplish my good will."

I began to look back over my life from the time I went to college to study for the ministry until that present time. I had been a student, a sexton at the church, and part of the church staff with ministry to shut ins. All of that was in what I then thought was my preparation to answer *the call*. Little did I know that the call had nothing to do with those things. That was all part of my works. No one is called to preach, or to pastor, or even to become a missionary. Those things are the works we do once we have answered *the call*. *The call* is to God for Him to use us as He sees necessary to accomplish His will and purpose. We are merely like pawns on a chess board. He has the right to move us around anyway He needs to get checkmate. If you read the Scriptures closely regarding the gifts of the ministry, you will find He does not refer to those gifts as callings. He uses the words *gave* and *appointed*. He gives pastors, teachers, prophets, etc. to the church for the edification of the church. To the church they are gifts. To those who exercise those gifts, it is their works.

Understanding this is so important to those who sense God saying to them, "I'm staking my claim on you," as He did to this young teenager years ago in that church camp. Don't confuse the works with *the call*. If He needs you to be a pastor for a while, do not believe that this is your life's calling. The call is to surrender to His divine will and purpose and be willing to do and to go wherever and whenever He leads you.

I would even go so far to say that in this context everyone who desires to be a Christ follower, a Christian, a disciple, or whatever definition you want to give it, must accept *the call.* We may have different roles to play, but we are all called to represent Him and complete the task of why He came to earth. Whether you are a pastor, a janitor, an accountant, or any other number of secular jobs, if you are truly following Christ, then you are called. Allow Him to move you wherever He needs you on the chess board of life to get checkmate.

Chapter 18
It Is Well With My Soul

"Give all your worries and cares to God, for He cares about you" (1 Peter 5:7).

I desperately need sleep, but I have been lying in bed with the thoughts I am about to share running through my mind. I must put them in writing before they leave my memory with the danger of not returning. I have learned when God is *nudging* me that I need to respond.

Sometimes life presents us with things that quite frankly just make us not even want to live anymore. A little over three years ago my wife lost her only two sons in a span of just eleven months. All I could do was watch as this beautiful person who had been so full of life was reduced to a fetal position as she fought her way to find a new normal in her life. The old normal will never return, but there must be a new one to continue living. It is essential to re-joining the human race and being there for those who still love and need her.

These past three years as I have witnessed her search to find answers to *why* when in simplest terms, there are none. That search is futile this side of heaven. I have prayed a lot during these three years for some wisdom, some verse from the Bible that would make sense of it all, but to no avail. It just seemed it was impossible to ever overcome that kind of pain. No escaping or overcoming it. Is it really possible to overcome that kind of anxiety in our lives when life goes horribly wrong? The answer is a resounding "yes!"

Yesterday morning I was listening to Chip Ingram speak about anxiety when he quoted the words to the song, *It Is Well with My Soul.* Many of us know the words well.

"When peace like a river attendeth my way,
 When sorrows like sea billows roll,
Whatever my lot, Thou hast taught me to say
It is well, it is well with my soul."

The words of this verse sound nice, but the power of them lies in the story behind the man who wrote them. They were written by a man named Horatio Spafford. He had been a very successful businessman who had amassed a fortune through investments. He lost it all in the Great Chicago Fire of 1871. If you have ever been so broke that you didn't know what was going to happen to you and your family, then you can understand what this broke man was going through. He worked hard to regain some sense of financial stability. At some point he decided that he needed to get away with his wife and four daughters just to focus as a family and pray about new direction in life. He had purchased tickets to travel by ship to Europe but at the last minute he was delayed because of a business deal that was in jeopardy. He sent his wife and daughters on with the intent of taking another ship to meet up with them later. There was a problem at sea and the ship went down. He received a telegram from his wife that read, "Saved…alone." He had just lost his four daughters. He had lost his fortune and now all four children are gone forever. Horatio booked another ship to take him to his wife as quickly as possible. When they reached the place where his wife's ship went down the captain called him to join him on deck. He pointed out to Horatio that this was the location where he lost his daughters. While standing there he penned those words, "When peace like a river attendeth my way, when sorrows like sea billows roll, it is well, it is well with my soul." How is that even possible? No, is that even possible amid such devastating circumstances? The answer for Horatio was "yes," and it can be for you too if you want it to be.

Nobody wants to live with that kind of heaviness of heart; going to bed at night only to get back up at 1am because sleep won't come. Your thoughts are spinning out of control, your heart is racing, the feeling of needing to throw up, and total weakness takes over your body. You cry out, wanting to die, when what you really want is just for the madness to stop. You want your life back, but don't know how to get it. You want it to be well with your soul!

We try all kinds of things to block out the pain and the fear. We go to bed and stay all day and night. We isolate and shut others out, so we don't have to pretend to be okay, or to listen to hollow attempts to make us feel better. We take pills to numb the pain or drink enough alcohol that we don't feel anything for a few hours. But no matter what we try, the pain doesn't stay away.

The one thing we don't do is turn to the One who can help. The one who begs us to cast our cares upon Him, because He cares for us. We begin to discover the secret to overcoming our grief and anxiety in John 15 where Jesus says: *"I am the true vine, and you are the branches. ...I have loved you even as the Father has loved me, ...remain in my love. ...I have told you these things so that you will be filled with my joy. ...Yes, your joy will overflow."* The key to overcoming our grief is found by living attached to the true vine. When we are truly living (connected) to Christ we can expect that our lives will be filled with joy, even amid a cruel and troubled world. Jesus goes on to say in John 16: *"Here on earth you will have many trials and sorrows. But take heart because I have overcome the world."*

When we live each day connected to the True Vine, we learn that we can give our sorrow, our fears over to a God who loves us and trust that He truly has our best interest at heart. We may not always understand the *why*, but we have the assurance that the *Who* holds us in the palm of His hand. Listen to how Paul lays it out in Philippians 4:6-7: *"Don't worry about anything; instead, pray about everything. Tell God what you need and thank Him for all He has done. Then, you will experience God's peace, which exceeds anything we can understand. His peace will guard your hearts and mind as you live in Christ Jesus. "*

The only way we can even understand the truth of this type of peace and joy is to abide in the True Vine. It sounds like foolishness to those who are not connected to the Vine. If you are struggling with sorry, fear, anger, and depression, I beg you to become truly connected to that Vine which is Jesus Christ. You will find that He truly cares for you.

Chapter 19
Freedom

"Jesus said to the people who believe in Him, you are truly my disciples if you remain in my teachings. And you will know the truth, and the truth will set you free. ...So, if the Son sets you free, you are truly free" (John 8: 31-32, 36).

Here is one of those rare moments where I prefer the King James text which says: *"If the Son sets you free, you are free indeed."* That word *indeed* is a little more emphatic, almost like an exclamation point!

Do you know what it is like to live in freedom? Do you feel imprisoned by the weight of living in a broken world? Do you want to be set free? Well, there is good news. Jesus tells us here that He came not only to forgive our sin, but to offer us complete freedom in every aspect of life, and even in death.

Let me give context to these verses. I hope you will read past the next few sentences to discover what real freedom is all about. But first I must call attention to what is required on our part to live in that freedom. It seems when I write about *our part* is when I get very little feedback or comments, but it is part of the package, and I can't ignore it. Jesus is speaking to those who have believed His message and been *obedient* to follow Him. Freedom is promised to all who do.

There comes a time when we will be faced with our own mortality. You make a trip to your doctor, and you hear him say the word cancer, or perhaps tumor. This is followed by the word inoperable. There is a whole host of emotions that will follow that and very quickly the first question comes to your mind, how long?

Imagine an inmate sitting on death row in the local prison. He has exhausted all his appeals; no governor's pardon is coming, and his execution is only minutes away. There is no hope left for such an individual. The time has arrived for him to be held accountable for the life he chose to live.

For the Christ-follower we see that earthly death has a totally different ending. Actually, it isn't an ending at all, it is a new beginning! It will be then that you recognize just how valuable your freedom in Christ will be. Paul speaks to this in 1 Corinthians 15: 55-58: *"Oh death, where is thy sting? O grave where is thy victory? The sting of death is sin; and the strength of sin is the law. But thanks be to God, which giveth us the victory through our Lord Jesus Christ."* You have been set free!!

Recognizing that the ultimate freedom comes to the Christ-follower upon the end of life here, there is also a life of freedom to be lived here and now. For over thirty-five years, I had the privilege of working with men struggling with addiction issues. Most people have very little understanding of the complexity of that word *addiction*; the broken homes, the being shunned by family, the loss of health, shelter, financial support, self-esteem, and so much more. Usually by the time they walked into our doors, any sense of freedom was gone. They had become prisoners to that lifestyle with very little hope of a better life. With those that I counseled (discipled). I began with the message that Christ can set you free, and if you let Him, you will be free indeed!

It wasn't easy and I wish I could tell you that a hundred percent of them were set free, but that just wasn't the case. Most simply did not want to hear about *our part*. They wanted the reward of freedom, but no discipline to follow the teachings of Christ to get it. Those teachings are there, not for the purpose of binding us up to a set of rules or regulations, but for the purpose of setting us free. For those men, it would mean giving Christ a chance to prove He meant what he said about freedom. After all, at this point in life what else did they have to lose? It meant a willingness on their part to quit using the drugs and alcohol that were killing their minds and bodies. Within a few months, they gained weight, their health began to improve, and their self-confidence began to return. Freedom had already begun to set in, although most of them did not credit it to God, but rather to their own effort. Yes, they did the work, and it was the hardest work anyone ever must face in dealing with the demons of addiction. But the freedom came from Christ, just as He promised.

Now the real test was about to begin. One that would ultimately decide if complete freedom would come, or if they would lose it and slip back into the prison of addiction. For some it meant mending things with family; others would have to be willing to face up to outstanding warrants and risk jail time. In many instances the judge commuted their sentences, but for others it meant serving out their sentence behind bars, which doesn't sound like freedom, does it? But, by their willingness to follow Christ, freedom was right around the corner. I have been there to pick them up when they walked out of the prison gates: no more looking over their shoulders, no more outstanding warrants, no more facing jail time. Now they were beginning to understand the importance of following Christ and the result was at that moment they had been set free indeed! From that point on they had a choice to live in that freedom or quit trusting God's way and return to the pig pen of addiction.

For the Christ-follower it may be much more subtle than the illustration I just gave of the addict. Freedom may come in the form of a sexually transmitted disease that never developed, or a broken home and marriage that never occurred.

Here is a definition of freedom in Christ from the OpenBible.org: *The ability to fulfill one's destiny, to function in terms of one's ultimate goal. In* other words, Christ death on the Cross has freed you to become the person your Creator designed you to be.

I first surrendered to Christ when I was only fifteen. I wish I could say I have lived in that freedom He promised since that night at youth camp, but that would be far from the truth. I was always close to my father as a little boy. As a little boy I was always referred to as *Clay's boy*. Since that was my father's name, I was proud to be referred to that way. My father and I were really close, and I loved hanging out with him. I wish I could say that it remained that way until he passed away, but such is not the case. When I was thirteen, he was diagnosed with terminal cancer. His fate turned out to be three years of horrible pain and agony. As the pain grew increasingly worse, and as he began to fail, my own emotions and mental health seemed to be attached to his pain and fifteen. He was so proud of me. He immediately went out and bought me my first Bible. I still have it to this day. It will be buried with me. But the more he suffered the more I suffered. As tempted as I am to go into the details it would simply take too long to put it in a short devotion. Suffice to say, I became angry at what life was giving me. Angry at my dad because he was sick and not able to be my dad. Angry at God for not healing my dad, and angry at others who were enjoying a normal life with their families, which I was not. I was imprisoned by that anger and bitterness for years. It was sealed for me when my home church passed judgement on me and turned their back on me when I needed them the most. This has affected me to this day as I still have issues with what I refer to as *organized religion*. That is another topic I will address soon, if God allows. Finally, in my late twenty's I cried out to God. Here was my simple prayer: "God, I have really messed up. I am sick with anger. I am losing everything that means anything to me. I can't ask you to take away my problems, I do not deserve it. But Lord, if you will just get me through it I will devote the rest of my life to you." At 2 am, on the hood of my car, freedom came that night. There have been times when I have failed to walk in it and had to adjust in order not to lose it, but I was set free that early morning, and I am free indeed!

I leave you with a passage found in 1 Peter 2:16-17: *"Live as people who are free, not using your freedom as a cover-up for evil, but living as servants of God. Honor everyone."*

Chapter 20
Planting Seeds

"The Kingdom of God is like the farmer who scatters seeds on the ground. Night and day whether he is asleep or awake, the seeds sprout and grow, but he does not understand how it happens" (Mark 4:26-27).

I realize that this might change the context of this passage, but if I were to do a modern-day version it would sound something like this: "All believers are a part of the Kingdom of God, and this is what we do every day. We scatter seed, twenty-four hours a day. We don't even know we are scattering the seed, but it sprouts and grows anyway."

Although I have taken a lot of liberty in the way I have interpreted it, the fact remains that we are spreading seed all the time without even realizing it.

I have a vague but very fond memory of when I was a little boy of no more than four or five years old. My Mother would set me on her lap and sing to me until I would fall asleep. I learned what her favorite songs were after hearing them many, many times. I can hear her now singing, "I come to the garden alone, while the dew is still on the roses, ... and He walks with me and He talks with me, and He tells me I am His own." How I would love to have her here to sing that to me one more time. As that little boy, I would imagine what it would be like to really meet Jesus in a garden and walk with Him. What would it really be like to hear Jesus speak to me? I thought of that song a lot during my years of growing up. As you can see, I am nearing the twilight years of my life and I still think of it. My mother had no idea when she was singing to me as a little boy that she was planting a seed. She was just trying to get her little boy to sleep. Little did she know that seed would one day sprout and grow in my heart making me want to follow that Jesus until I hear His voice for real.

To say that I loved my dad would be a big understatement. Growing up, he was my hero. (I confess that once he became ill and I knew he was dying, my grief and anger caused me to fail him as a worthy son.) I am not sure if I will see my father again in heaven or not. This is one time that I pray that my theological understanding of Scripture is wrong. He was a good man, and although he never went to church, he was baptized a few months before he passed away. There were two seeds that he planted in my life. The first one was shortly after I gave my life to Christ as a fifteen-year-old boy. He bought me my first Bible. It wasn't just any Bible; it was a Scofield Reference Bible. At the age of fifteen, it was beyond my comprehension how to use it. But He knew that as time passed, I would learn to use it, and I did. I still have that Bible to this day; with all kinds of scribbled notes, I have written through the years. The seed that he planted in this teenager's life sprouted into the spiritual person I have become today.

The other seed that he planted came during the final year of his life. He would always talk about *next year* in terms of spending time with me. Looking back, it is now clear to me that he wanted me to know that being with me meant something. We were big fishing buddies. During that final year he would say, "son, if the good Lord is willing, next year we are going to go deep sea fishing." Sadly, next year never came. But he had planted a seed that has sprouted in multiple ways. I cannot add up the countless hours I have spent reading Scripture about the Lord's will, trying to grasp the meaning of it. All my father was doing, or so he thought, was to express his desire for one more fishing trip with his son. Little did he know at the time that he had planted a seed in my life that would one day sprout into that teenage boy's life with a desire to know the will of God. I think of that statement every time I am asked to speak to someone about God's will. And it usually is at a time of loss in their lives, like the loss I felt as a teenager losing his earthly idol.

The point of all of this is that we are planting seeds in people's lives every day, usually without even knowing it. It can be good seed or bad seed. The least we need to do is be aware we are doing it. It will temper all our actions and words if we can just be conscious of that fact. As we are raising our children, or playing with our grandchildren, unbeknown to us we are planting seeds. It doesn't stop with just family. That co-worker who may not know the Lord is watching the seed you sow that may someday, without you even knowing it, may sprout to bring him or her to know Christ for themselves, or keep them from coming to Christ.

Every day I realize that my neighbors, some of whom I know well, others who I simply know well enough to wave at when we pass, are seeing the seed that I am spreading from my life. Will it be good seed that grows in such a way that it brings light into their life? I most likely will never know.

You see, it is one of the laws of nature that all of life was meant to reproduce. For that to happen seeds must be planted. So, whether we know it, or even if we would rather not, our life is sowing seeds every day. Fruit will come of it without you even knowing it. The only question that remains is what type of seed are we spreading?

We are all farmers who are spreading seed every day, every night. Without knowing how, the seed sprouts and grows. In that context, instead of asking what kind of seed we are planting, maybe the question should be, what kind of fruit will it produce?

Chapter 21
Constant Contact

"Devote yourselves to prayer with an alert mind and a thankful heart" (Colossians 4:2).

Two nights ago, my wife and I were both awakened by what we thought was a noise inside the place where we were staying. After a thorough search both inside and outside, only to find nothing there, I decided to stay up for a while *just in case*. It was then I heard my phone alert me of an incoming message from West Africa. A fifteen-month-old boy had fallen into a pot of boiling water and needed immediate medical attention. In many developing countries like parts of Africa, if you want medical attention you must pay in advance. If you have no money, you will be turned away. His family had no money for his treatment, and they needed it immediately. Without it, the little boy most assuredly would have died. Then I realized that the noise we heard wasn't a noise at all, but rather a *nudge* from God. I was overcome with emotion that God could get our attention in the middle of the night and use us to intervene on this baby's behalf on the other side of the world. That is what an alert mind can do when God needs us, and my heart was more than thankful that God called on us to intercede for this child because He knew He could get our attention.

Paul's directive here is one of constant and loyal contact with God, a call to constant prayer. Prayer is not just an event where from time to time I *talk to God*. It is much more than that. It is a constant open line of communication between us and God. 1 Thessalonians 5:17 clarifies this expectation with these words: *"pray without ceasing."* Another translation says, *"pray without end."*

A phrase often used in different context is *keep the line of communication open*. In difficult times of marriage as well as other domestic circumstances it is vital that the line of communication is still open. When communication stops, it means the end of the relationship. In military terms, it can mean the difference to winning or losing a war. Communication up and down the chain of command will determine if the battle is won or lost.

For a Christian, the implications are no different. Our relationship with God is directly impacted by how close and constant our contact is with Him. Without that constant contact, our relationship, at best, is distant and weak. We become up and down in our faith in Him as a result. Our faith is good and strong if things are going well. But with adversity it becomes weak, and we struggle to keep what little faith we have. In worst case scenarios, we lose our faith all together. In forty years of ministry, I have counseled many couples and realized even before they did, that the relationship was over and that divorce was inevitable, simply because the line of communication was cut off. I have witnessed the same in people's relationship with God. They had what I would describe as a religious knowledge and belief in God, but there was no closeness, no constant contact in the relationship where intimate trust and faith could thrive. When the battles of life confronted them, they would have no hope of winning those battles. They would have no hope of victory, no joy unspeakable, no living life more abundantly, all which Christ promised us. It isn't because He broke His promise or lied to us; it is rather because we don't really know Him well enough to completely trust that He has our best interest at the center of His heart. You will never achieve the victorious life through a religious knowledge or practicing religious principles and rituals. The kind of relationship that never fails us, that allows us to be on *speed dial* if He needs us, can only be experienced by being in a state of never ceasing prayer with an alert mind and a thankful heart.

How do we come to a place where we actually experience that kind of closeness and intimacy with God? How do we achieve a constant level of being in His presence? Two thoughts come to mind.

1) You must desire to have it. Desire is defined as a state of mind expressed by wanting, wishing, longing, or craving for something. I like the last definition *craving for something*. Would you consider yourself a person who *craves* to be constantly in the presence of the Lord? This is where it starts. Without that longing or craving, we are making the decision to have a religious experience rather than the personal relationship in which God created us for. When the battles of life come, those times in life where tragedy strikes, a religious experience will always fail you. It is only a real and personal relationship with God that can sustain you.

It has been almost two years now since I started each day asking God to allow me to see with the eyes of Christ, hear with the ears of Christ, and speak with the words of Christ. It would take more time than allowed in a devotion to tell you what a difference that one desire has made in my life. Another thing I have learned about desire is that it will drive you toward action. It happens every day in our lives. Think about it in terms of a young person who feels that they have met that *Mr. or Mrs. Right*. We find different reasons and ways to be in their presence. It plays out in the way we dress, the way we act, and even the perfume or cologne we wear. Maybe the most important factor is we seem to always be conscience of the way we conduct ourselves. When we desire that kind of relationship with God, it plays out in our spiritual lives as well. We go from *I know I should spend more time praying to God,*" to one of always wanting to be constantly in His presence. That is the definition of real prayer.

I cannot stand to be alone. I always want to be with my wife. She can be in another part of the house for hours at a time and I am just fine. I may not physically see her or talk to her for a few hours at a time, but I know she is there with me. We may go on a long trip and not say a word for long periods of time as we travel, but she is there in my presence. I can hear her if she speaks. I can reach out and touch her anytime I desire. We spend so much time together that we know what the other one is thinking before we even speak. We know each other's likes and dislikes and will bend over backwards to please one another. That is what desire drives you to do with someone you want to be with. That is why God created you and me. To be in that kind of relationship with Him. Anything less is just religious *window dressing*, what Paul describe as a *"noisy gong, or a clanging cymbal."* Jesus referred to the difference in a religious experience and a spiritual relationship with these words, *"Outwardly you look like righteous people, but inwardly you are filled with dead bones"* (Matthew 23:27).

2.) You must be *"connected to the Vine."* Again, Jesus used this illustration to speak about our relationship with Him: *"I am the true Vine ... Abide in me and I in you"* (John 15:1. 4). The two most important words that Jesus speaks here are *"Remain,"* which means to stay connected to the Vine, and *"in,"* which means exactly what it says. He wants us to stay connected and live *in* the power of the Vine which is Christ himself. Anything less withers and dies. The key to *constant contact* with Christ is staying connected to the Vine. No spiritual life is possible outside of that.

In summary, these verses are about praying with an alert mind, praying without ceasing, and being connected *in* the Vine. All come together to show us how to stay in "constant contact" with Christ. Now the only thing that remains is to answer the question, what is it that you desire in knowing Christ? What is it that you crave? You already know what God desires or craves as it relates to you. He loved you so much He gave His son to die for you (John 3:16). The choices are simple; no relationship with Jesus at all, a religious experience void of true relationship, or abiding *in* Christ and He abiding *in* you which leads to His constant presence in your life.

As I inventory my life journey, I can account for all three of these choices at different times of my life. Now that I have arrived at *abiding in Christ and He is abiding in me* and have experienced what that is like, I would never go back, and neither would you. Choose wisely.

Chapter 22
God's Rejects

"Jesus replied, 'I am the bread of life. Whoever comes to me will never be hungry again. Whoever believes in me will never be thirsty. ... However, those the Father has given me will come to me, and I will never reject them" (John 6:35 and 37).

When I was in the eighth grade, we had a new kid at school. His name was Timmy. He was a couple of grades ahead of me, but our school was small, and everyone knew each other. It wouldn't have mattered though because Timmy really stood out, not for his good looks or personality, but for all the negative traits he possessed. Timmy was not someone pleasant to look at. He had this huge nose that seemed wide enough to cover most of his face. He had acne so bad that you would really have to search for a smooth section of skin His hair was thick, and always dirty; only God would know when it last had a comb or brush in it. His pants and shirts were always wrinkled, torn, and never fit right. He wore a belt about three sizes too big and the extra length of it always hung somewhere around his knees. So here I am some fifty-six years after my eighth-grade encounter with Timmy and you can see I still have a good grasp of poor Timmy. But as much as I remember about him, that is not what I think about when I think of him. What draws emotion from me was how the older boys treated him. They laughed at him and made fun of his looks. Snide comments were made all the time about his personal looks as well as the way he was dressed. All this added up to frequent fights from his classmates. Actually, you must have two people involved to have a fight, and Timmy would just stand there and take it, always leaving the scene with his clothes torn and bloodied from the beating he had been given. I can only imagine the emotional pain Timmy must have carried from those beatings, which no doubt hurt much more than the physical pain he was experiencing. I have wondered many times whatever happened to Timmy. Did he find a way to grow up and be *normal?* Did he find a way out of his poverty? Did the weight of it all cause him to take his life? I will never know those answers as we moved the following year and I have never heard anything more about him. Poor Timmy was what some would call a reject of society.

If you have ever experienced rejection in your life, then you know it is painful. Your situation may not be the same as Timmy's, but the pain is just as real. There are those children who have experienced the pain of their parents' divorce. Rejection is often the emotion that the child feels as a result. It is just the nature of a simple child to think that if mommy or daddy are leaving then they must not love me anymore. The same can be said of the husband or wife when their partner announces that they are leaving the marriage. Then there are those who have grown up poor, the ones who have not had the opportunity for a good education, the excluded ones from the *cliques* at work and society. What about those with physical or mental handicaps who get stared at any time they go out in public? For the most part, they feel like they are the rejects of society. We all have known someone like that in our lives. Maybe you even feel that way about yourself.

Jesus understood what it was like to be rejected. Listen to what the Prophet Isaiah said about Him in Isaiah 53:3: *"He was despised and rejected, a man of sorrows, acquainted with deepest grief. We turned our backs on Him and looked the other way. He was despised and we did not care."* Even as I typed this out, I cannot help but think this is exactly what I did to my eighth-grade classmate Timmy. I turned my back and did nothing to help him. How much more rejected could that have made him feel, that not one person came to his defense? And in the case of Christ who was going to give His life for those who rejected Him, how much more rejected could he feel? Enough to experience the *deepest grief* apparently.

Here is the *good news*. God does not have any rejects. Having been one Himself I have no doubt that He has a special place in His heart for all who have felt the pain of rejection, including me. If you have ever felt the pain of rejection, or perhaps even feeling it as you are reading this, there is One who understands and feels your grief at the very deepest level. He calls out and says: *"Come to me if you are burdened with heaviness, take my yoke, and give me yours. I will give you rest and lift you up, I will never reject you* (Matthew 11:29 Richard Williams translation).

Chapter 23
The Seasons of Life

"For everything there is a season, a time for everything under heaven. A time to be born and a time to die. A time to plant and a time to harvest. A time to kill and a time to heal. A time to tear down and a time to build up. A time to cry and a time to laugh. A time to grieve and a time to dance" (Ecclesiastes 3: 1-8).

This passage of Scripture came to me as I was preparing for my sister's memorial service this past week. I thought back to my early childhood when we would travel from Arkansas to Kansas to visit my sister and her family. I would always be filled with anticipation as I would have the opportunity to play with my two nephews who both happened to be older than their Uncle Richard. I also vaguely remember when my sister gave birth to two additional children, making me a proud uncle to four nephews before the age of six! Then there were the times that they would take a vacation and come to our house. I cherished those the most because that would mean fishing trips with my dad where we always caught dozens of fish. Like many of you who are reading this, we all have fond memories of our childhood. Memories of playing with childhood friends, special trips with family, or maybe a favorite swimming hole. I must at this point pay tribute to Loretta Downing who gave me my first kiss after a daring game of *spin the bottle*. My head was spinning, my heart racing, and I couldn't breathe for three days after that!

Memories like these are special in our lives. They certainly were to me. I now understand the term, *the good old days*. That was the first season of our lives. I call it the season of childhood for the lack of a better term. Those were the years that would shape us for the other seasons of life to follow.

That first season of life is far more important than what we may have realized as a child going through it. The author, Robert Fulghum wrote a book titled, *All I Need to Know I Learned in Kindergarten.* The premise of his book is that the world would be a better place if adults would live by the principles we learned in that season of life, i.e., sharing, being kind to one another, cleaning up after themselves, and living a balanced life of work, play, and learning. We also learned the difference between right and wrong. We quickly picked up what type of behaviors got the most desired response from our parents. For instance, as an infant if we were hungry, we would cry and scream to the top of our lungs until someone stuck a bottle in our mouth. The same behavior worked well if our diapers were dirty, or if we were sleepy, as well as a lot of other demands we might have. We learned the definition of *yes* and *no*, and depending on our parents' child raising style, we learned if *no* meant *no*, or if it just meant keep asking until they say *yes*. That first season of life would most definitely be the season where I would develop my character that would be with me through all the other seasons of my life.

Next would come the season of discovering for ourselves who we really were, or perhaps wanted to be. We discovered what subjects in school drew us in, and which ones did not. I would learn where a lot of my natural ability came from. Did I have a natural gift for mathematics, or was science of more interest to me? Was I a natural at athletics? The answer to these questions would determine if we were off to college, or perhaps a Trade School. Or, if you were like me, you had a hard time figuring that out. But eventually we found our way and entered the season of adulthood.

On December 6, 2020, my sister passed from the season of life to the season of dying. That is another season that we will all face at some point in our lives. There is no skipping it, it is inevitable. The only choice we have as we pass into this season is where we will spend the following season that is to come. We talked about how important our first season of life is, because it is then that we form much of our character that would be with us throughout all the later seasons of life. This season of dying is as equally important. The outcome of this season of dying will be determined by how we lived our season of adulthood. Somewhere in that season of adulthood we were faced with our spirituality. Did I make the decision to trust in God and accept His Son as Lord, or did I join the masses and dismiss it as not being legitimate?

For those of us that my sister left behind, we entered a season of grieving that began at her passing. There is no right or wrong way to grieve, nor a specific time limit on how long it will last. Grief is different for each of us, and that is normal and okay.

Grieving is an area where I have had a lot of experience. First, losing my dad when I was only fifteen, followed by losing both my brothers in their thirty's, and finally my mom. All of them asked the same thing of me during that season of their lives. That was to keep the family together and to watch out for each other. It is during this season of life where many families drift apart, or just out of being so busy with life, fail to keep the family relationships close and meaningful. I want to encourage you not to lose the family unit whenever you face this season of life.

Then, one day we will come to the final season. It is when the end of our time here on earth is finished. I encourage you with the words of the Apostle Paul found in Colossians 3:1b: *"Set your eyes on the realities of Heaven, where Christ sits in the place of honor at God's right hand."*

To set your eyes on the reality of Heaven you must first believe that it is real. To believe that you must believe that Christ is who He said

He was. If that is a struggle you currently have, I beg you to private message me and let's discuss it. When I only have a moment, I like to use a phrase I picked up from my good friend Jim DiRado. "A man will give his life for something that he knows to be true and worth dying for, but no man will die for a lie." Jesus' disciples all laid down their lives for Christ and not one of them declared that He was a fraud! Start today setting your eyes on the reality of Heaven with the anticipation of a great family reunion one day in the not-too-distant future with those you love and who are waiting for you.

Chapter 24
Guarding Your Heart and Mind

"Don't worry about anything; instead pray about everything. Tell God what you need and thank Him for all He has done. Then you will experience God's peace, which exceeds anything we can understand. His peace will guard your hearts and minds as you live in Christ Jesus" (Philippians 4:6-7).

I used to have this passage taped to the dashboard of my car and would read it every time I went anywhere. My thoughts were not focused on *getting* things from God in a selfish way. Instead, I would think through my work schedule for the day and pray for what I would need to be successful with whatever was on my agenda. I found it amazingly true as I would recall the things that God had already provided in my life, that a sense of peace would come over me as I remembered them. The night I knelt beside my daughter, and she prayed for God to make her well and keep her well always loomed large in remembering God's supplying my needs. Each time I would think back to the time that God supplied me a new pair of shoes always brought a smile to my face. It was more than just a sense of peace that I experienced; it was a confidence that *"God would supply all my needs according to the riches of His glory in Christ Jesus"* (Philippians 4:19). I have had more than a few meetings in my life that would be considered serious and stressful. The act of thanking Him for past victories always gave me the confidence and peace that I would not face the day alone. That Scripture would still be attached to the dash of my car had my car not been stolen. That event is now added to the things that I thank God for doing. There was a $15,000.00 check endorsed setting above the sun visor. When the car was finally recovered the check was still there.

Recently my thoughts have expanded to the final sentence of verse seven: *"His peace will guard your hearts and minds as you live in Christ Jesus."* Paul's emphasis has changed from God providing for our needs to guarding our heart and mind, as well as *living* in Christ.

Why did Paul emphasis the heart and mind? Why not just repeat the words of Isaiah 26:3; *"You will keep in perfect peace those whose minds are steadfast, because they trust You."* Why did he specifically refer to the mind and heart?

The answer to the question is quite simple. The heart and mind represent the whole of who I am. If someone does something that hurts my feelings, I don't feel it in my elbow, I feel it in my heart. If we get rejected by someone we dearly love, we do not feel that in our big toe, the hurt is in the heart. In regard to our minds, it is no different. If someone spreads vicious lies about us, the thought of retaliation does not come from my left leg, or my thoughts of how to even the score don't come from my fingers or toes. That all comes from my mind. Everything but the heart and mind is just the packaging that houses me. The heart and mind represent the spirit and soul that last forever. That is the part of me that lives on long after my physical body returns to the dust of the earth.

Solomon penned the words of Proverbs 23:7: *"So as a man thinketh in his heart, so is he."* Do we think with our heart or our mind? The simple answer would be that we think with our mind, not with our heart. However, Solomon in his wisdom, realized that the two were connected. Whatever our mind thinks, it is the heart that forms the emotions that correspond with those thoughts. They are inter-connected. They cannot live apart from one another. If your heart stops the brain dies, or if the brain quits functioning, the heart stops beating.

When Paul tells us that God will guard our hearts and minds, we must see it from two perspectives. The first is while I am here on earth. We live in a very broken world where tragedies abound, where sin runs rampant. We face it every day where we work; it attacks us in our homes with our husbands and wives, or through our children. Finally, it has found its way into the church. Things we once recognized as blatant sin are now considered acceptable. The only way we will ever overcome the tragedies of life or keep sin from infecting our heart and mind is to stay focused on allowing Christ to live in us. That is where our victory comes from; not in the news, or in the temporal answers it offers. It will not come with any amount of money. It will not come from the pleasures offered in television and magazines. It will not come from pills or from a bottle. It only comes by keeping our focus on the one who said: "*I have come to give life, and to give it more abundantly*" (John 10:10.)

Abundant living, perfect peace, only comes when my mind is laser focused on Jesus Christ. I have shared about the first time I was diagnosed with cancer and was filled with fear. I was so shaken by it that it took any semblance of life away from me. My second battle with the disease was different. I had a perfect peace that only continues to grow the closer I get to the end of this life. What is the difference? I learned to focus on the one who promised to never leave or forsake me. I learned to focus on Jesus Christ, and now the closer I come to the end of my life here on earth, the more I look forward with anticipation to seeing face to face, the Jesus of my focus.

That leads to the second perspective, eternity. As believers we should realize that our eternal life has already begun. It is not something that happens after we die. The only thing that happens after we die is that we move from one location to the next. But the things of heaven are available to us now. If our minds are focused on Jesus, we have access to a God who will wipe aways all our tears, where darkness cannot overtake the light in our lives. We have access to a God who will never leave us or forsake us. He will guard our hearts and minds right now, if our mind is fixed on Him.

Chapter 25
Stones of Separation

"Now a certain man, Lazarus was sick… therefore his sisters sent for Jesus saying, Lord, behold, he whom thou lovest is sick. When Jesus heard that he said, 'This sickness is not unto death, but for the glory of God. That the Son of God might be glorified thereby.' …When He had heard therefore that he was sick, He abode still in the same place where He was. Then after that He saith unto His disciples, 'Let us go into Judea again. …Our friend Lazarus sleepeth; but I go that I may wake him out of sleep.' Jesus therefore again groaning within himself cometh to the grave. It was a cave, and a stone lay upon it. Jesus said, 'take ye away the stone.' Martha, the sister of him who was dead, saith unto Him, 'Lord, by this time he stinketh; for he hath been dead four days!' Jesus saith unto her, 'Said I not unto thee that if thou wouldest believe, thou shouldest see the glory of God?' Then they took away the stone from the place where the dead was laid. …and Jesus lifted up His eyes, and said, 'Father, I thank thee that thou hast heard me. And I knew that thou hearest me always. But because of the people which stand by I said it, that they may believe that thou hast sent me'" (John 11:1-44 KJV).

Somewhere during Christ's journey here on earth, he met and became close friends with this man Lazarus and his two sisters, Mary and Martha. Their relationship was far more than casual. They were very much like family.

Lazarus had become terminally ill, and the two sisters sent a messenger pleading with Christ to hurry and come to heal their brother before it is too late. Knowing the closeness of their relationship, Mary and Martha must have been perplexed at the delay in Jesus' response. Christ was about a day's journey away, thus taking the messenger a day to arrive with the news. Instead of rushing to His best friends' side, He waited two more days before beginning the trip back to where Lazarus was. Christ made the statement that this was so the people would see *the glory of God.* When He finally arrived, we find that Lazarus had been dead now for four days. Martha rushed to meet Christ, but Mary stays back. Christ calls for Mary and they all travel to the burial tomb together. Jesus made a request that the stone be removed, and they argued that it was too late, and Lazarus would be rotting and stinking by this time. Finally, they listen to Christ and removed the stone. The very next thing that happened was that Christ paused, looked to heaven and prayed to His Father these words: *"Father, thank you that you have heard me."* Then, and only then, Jesus called for Lazarus to come out and Jesus spoke these words: *"loose him and let him go free!"*

For as long as I can remember this event has been proclaimed as the greatest miracle contained within the New Testament. Perhaps that is true, but there was something else that happened that day that was at least just as important, and maybe even more so. It happened after they had arrived at the tomb but before Christ raised Lazarus from the dead. The scene was this. The people were grieving the death of their friend and close family member. They were upset that Christ did not come when He was called for and they had resigned themselves to the fact that the one they loved was dead. The question on everyone's mind was, why did Christ allow it? As a result, it was natural that they would not want to remove the stone that lay between them and Lazarus. It was over. Finally, they surrendered to Christ's request, and they removed the stone. You would think that the next thing that Christ would do would be to rescue Lazarus, but instead He looked to heaven and said: *"Father thank you that You have heard me."* This seems to indicate that Jesus had been praying to His Father for something. But what could it be He needed to pray about? Christ already knew He would raise Lazarus from the dead. He stated that before He even began His journey four days before. He affirmed it again upon arrival by saying: *"If you just believe, you will see the glory of God!"* So, what could He have been praying for? It seems obvious to me. There was a role for the people to play that day, to *"take the stone away."* They resisted, and Christ had to convince them to take it away. He could have just pointed a finger at the stone and pulverized it; something I might do for a dramatic affect. When it is finally removed, it seems that Christ is giving a sigh of relief for answered prayer: *"thank you Father for hearing me"*...whew! I am personally convinced that had they not been willing to remove the stone, life for Lazarus would have been over. Their willingness to remove the stone was that vital.

So, what does all this have to do with us today? Life in this broken world is hard. Things happen that we don't understand, as they did not understand on that day at the tomb. Where was Christ when we needed Him? Bad things happen to good people and when they do, sometimes we have stones that get rolled into our hearts that begin to eat away at our faith in God. For me, one of those stones happened at the loss of my father when I was a teenager and needed him at a critical time of my life. Another stone was rolled into my heart when I had the painful experience with my pastor and church family passing judgement on me. Anger and bitterness began to erode my soul as sure as decay begins to rot the human body. Some experience painful divorce, children feel the abandonment of a parent, others receive the news of a crippling and even terminal disease that has invaded the body. And the worst of all, like Mary and Martha, we experience the loss of a loved one. All of these can cause *stones of separation* to come between our hearts and God. When that happens, we slowly begin to die emotionally and spiritually. Christ is still praying that we will *take the stones away.* Rather than blaming Him, He wants us to trust Him. Our role today is still the same as it was that day at the tomb of Lazarus. We must do our part to remove the stones of life so that we can see and live in the *glory of God!* Do you have any stones that have rolled into your life? Stones of anger, pain, doubt, blame, or even hate toward others or God? If you would just remove those stones, Jesus would command for you the same as He did for Lazarus, LOOSE HIM AND LET HIM GO FREE!!!"

Chapter 26
A Broken Heart

"Purify me from my sins, and I will be clean; wash me, and I will be whiter than snow. Oh, give me back my joy again; You have broken me- now let me rejoice. Don't keep looking at my sins. Remove the stain of my guilt. Create in me a clean heart, oh God. Renew a loyal spirit within me. Do not banish me from Your presence, and don't take Your Holy Spirit from me. Restore to me the joy of your salvation and make me willing to obey You" (Psalms 51: 7-12).

I have been wrestling with what I wanted to say about this Psalm for days now. Each time I begin to write there are so many thoughts, and so many different implications contained within it. But let me make a feeble attempt at what led me to this particular passage.

It is not unusual for someone to reach out to me, wanting to talk, or ask a question as it pertains to their relationship with God. Not too long ago, someone who was obviously distraught, did reach out. He was so distraught he could barely form sentences between the sobs and tears coming down his cheeks. He had been struggling with what he described as a sin from his past that was so egregious that he thought God could never forgive him.

This is exactly where David found himself after having committed murder, when he penned these words: *"Forgive me for shedding blood, oh God who saves, then I will joyfully sing of Your forgiveness. Unseal my lips oh Lord, that my mouth may praise You. You do not desire a sacrifice, or I would offer one. You do not want a burnt offering. The sacrifice you desire is a broken spirit. You will not reject a broken and repentant heart."* What the person who had sought me out was failing to recognize was the fact that their brokenness was the very reason God had already forgiven them. David addressed an important point when it comes to seeking forgiveness from God for the sin in our lives. Religious ritual will not get the job done. Even a prayer, in and of itself, is not enough. David, no doubt, had performed the ritual of sacrifices many times in His life. But this time, the blood of bulls and goats were useless. It is no different today. We may go to church, read our Bibles, and say our prayers, but when it comes to the forgiveness of our sin, nothing short of a crushed spirit, and a broken heart will suffice.

I am not talking about the kind of broken heart we feel when we suffer loss. I have counseled many who have suffered through broken marriages, or the loss of a newborn child, and others who have buried their loved ones. That brokenness is real and runs deep. We never really get over it, but we learn to adjust and make allowance for it.

There is a brokenness that is more painful and runs deeper than when we suffer loss. It is a brokenness that we feel when the cause of a loss is because of my actions. With reluctance I share just one example. A young mother who loved her child dearly had taken her eyes off that child for just a minute. In that minute when she was not looking, the child wandered away and was not found for three days. The child was found floating in a body of water less than a mile from their house. You do not have to blame the mother; she has enough blame for herself. She feels a brokenness that I pray you never experience. This is a special brokenness that happened in an instant but will last forever on this earth.

Jesus gave us the perfect example in Luke 18: *"The Pharisee prayed, 'thank you God that I am not like other people... I fast twice a week, and I give You a tenth of my income.' ... But the tax collector stood at a distance and dared not to even lift his eyes toward heaven as he prayed. Instead, he beat his chest in sorrow, saying, 'Oh God, be merciful to me, for I am a sinner.' I tell you this sinner, not the Pharisee, returned home justified before God."* It wasn't the prayer that made the difference, it was the sorrowful heart. That brokenness is what made the difference. The kind of brokenness we should feel at the realization that Christ's life was given because of our own sin. If you haven't felt that kind of brokenness toward Him, then you have never fully understood the sacrifice He made on your behalf.

There is so much more rich and important truth found in David's Psalm. I will only address one more of them for now. David cried out to God in verse 10: *"Create in me a clean heart oh God."* It wasn't enough for David to just have a forgiven heart. He was asking God to *create* something new, a heart that was pure and not one that had been stained by the ravages of sin.

So, to the person who spoke to me through the tears and the pain of brokenness, you are David, and you are the tax collector. God would say to you, "I see your sorrow. I see your brokenness. Return home. You are justified. Your sins are forgiven".

Chapter 27
Seek His Face

"If my people, who are called by my name, will humble themselves and pray and seek my face and turn from their wicked ways, then I will hear from heaven, and I will forgive their sin and will heal their land (2 Chronicles 7:14).

Several weeks ago, I felt compelled to write about 2 Chronicles 7:14 where God promised to heal our land if we would be willing to humble ourselves, seek His face, repent of our wicked ways, and then pray. I felt led to write about it because of the overall condition we find ourselves in our country. I am burdened about how far we have drifted from God, even those of us who claim Him as our Savior. If you read the verses correctly you will discover that God says: *"If my people, who are called by name,"* which means He is not asking for the whole country to humble and repent, but only His people. That should alarm us. It is up to those of us who claim Him as Lord and Savior to turn our country around. To do so, not by protesting or arguing with those who do not share our views, but by simply becoming humble, seeking His face, and repenting of *our* sins. God promised to do the rest.

I received feedback about that post from several readers. One of the comments was to have me explain what it meant to seek His face. I prayed over that request for over a week before I answered. I felt inadequate to give a good answer, so instead of posting it publicly I answered though private messenger. Since then, others have raised the same question. So, I have decided to respond with a new post. Please keep two things in mind. 1) I prefer to write from a personal perspective rather than a formal commentary style. I feel it brings me closer to those of you who take the time to read my post. 2) I really would appreciate hearing from you regarding what it means to you personally. I have learned from my years of experience that when one person gives the insight you get *part* of the meaning. When several people share, you often get the *whole* picture. Here is my follow-up post.

We need to understand that there are always two contexts in which Scripture is written and when reading the Bible, it is important to understand both. The first is the context of the time, circumstance in which it was written, and to whom it was written. The second context applies to us as we read it *today* and seek to understand how God would want us to apply it to our lives. I want to direct most of my comments toward that second context with the understanding that *"God is the same yesterday, today, and forever"* (Hebrews 13:8), and the Word of God *"continues to work in those who believe"* (1 Thessalonians 2:13).

God had spoken to king Solomon regarding the use of the temple which he had just finished building for the Lord. God, who is all knowing, already knew that Solomon would let pride and arrogance lead him away from what God intended for his life. Solomon would also fail to understand *whose temple it was*. It is in that context that God speaks to Solomon to warn him of the consequences that would result. Yet, even in the midst of that, God wanted to give Solomon the assurance that if he would repent, turn from his wicked ways, and seek His face, He (God) would forgive him and bring healing to the land (Israel) which Solomon ruled.

In today's context I can only speak to what that means to me. I think each of us must find our way to seeking the face of God individually.

I am a duck out of water when it comes to today's technology. I barely understand enough to *get by*. Rather than call, or use Zoom, I will jump on a plane and fly clear across the country to have a conversation with someone, if the outcome of that conversation has serious ramifications. I like to look people *eye to eye*. You can tell so much more about a person if you are looking at them face to face that you cannot get any other way. I have looked into the face of people who are hurting deeply and by simply looking at them I could feel the pain they were experiencing. I have looked into the face of the addicted and seen that blank stare of complete lostness in their heart and soul. I have had the difficult conversations with some, who by simply looking into their face, I could tell they were lying or trying to mislead me. But the look that I enjoy the most is when I look upon someone's face and see the look of joy and happiness. Maybe they just met the love of their life or had a new baby. Whenever you encounter that look upon someone's face, it will almost always draw a smile back from the one looking on because they can sense the happiness of the individual. So, whether it is sadness, deceit, fear, or excitement or joy, it will always cause us to react. What we are, what we are feeling is always written on our face.

In that context, God is asking us to know Him in a very intimate way; not in just some religious sense, but to really know Him, what He is like, what He is thinking, and even what He is feeling. The whole purpose for God's creating man in the beginning was to have fellowship with Him. He would *"come to the garden in the cool of the day"* just to be with Adam and Eve. If we truly believe that *"God is the same today as yesterday,"* then He still wants to walk with us as He did with them. There are many ways He encourages us to *seek His face*. The most intimate would certainly be spending time with Him in prayer. I can promise you that anyone who sincerely seeks to spend time praying, talking to God, will learn to know He is communicating back. It is not some nutty idea, or just the practice of religious fanatics.

Another way to *seek His face* is to read the Scriptures. Anyone who tells you that it is easy, at least in the beginning, is not being honest. But the more time you spend doing it the more you become hungry for it. I have found two things that motivate me to study the

Bible. 1) Start where any good book starts, at the beginning and realize that you are reading the history of who God is and how we got to where we are. I like to tell people; *I want to know what makes God tick.* 2) Find a translation that is easy to understand. We have come a long way since the days of King James.

If I practice a consistent prayer life, coupled with studying *who* God is in the Bible, I am, in essence, trying to *seek His face*, or to understand His heart. What is it that is important to Him? Why does He get angry sometimes? What breaks His heart? What gives Him joy? Why does He love me despite my failures? The more I practice this, the clearer His face becomes. The clearer that becomes, the more my desire to please Him grows. The more I grow, the more important it becomes that the people around me are not put off by it, but rather are drawn to it.

Seek His face! You will not be disappointed.

Chapter 28
Overcoming Temptations

"If you think you are standing strong, be careful not to fall. The temptations in your life are no different from what others experience. And God is faithful. He will not let the temptation be more than you can stand. When you are tempted, He will show you a way out so that you can endure" (1 Corinthians 10:12-13).

Last night I was sent a private message by someone who follows my devotional posts. He was struggling to understand the above verses. Although he did not specifically say, I felt that what he was really having trouble with was the last two sentences of verse 13: *"He will not let the temptation be more than you can stand. When you are tempted, He will show you a way out so that you can endure."* As a result, that was the perspective I took in my response. It is only a partial response and certainly could use further reflection. Here was my response and, as always, I invite you to comment with your own insight as well.

We all know in our heart the way that God wants us to live our lives. It is built into our DNA by Him as our Creator. Many have drifted so far from Him that it is hard to recognize anymore, but I assure you as one who used to be about as far from God as one could be, it is there, buried somewhere deep inside of you. Christ put it in very direct terms in John 14 when He said: *"if you love me, keep my commandments."* I could quote many more verses in the Bible that tell us how God wants us as His children to live out our lives. He tells us how we are to love others, how to forgive, and put others needs above our own. In light of allowing His own Son to die on our behalf, His expectation is that we love Him without conditions. He also tells us clearly the things we should not do that lead us into trouble in this life, and that leads to heartache and pain.

Satan knows that if he can cause or tempt us to not follow what God would want for us, it will affect our relationship and ultimately put a wedge between us and God.

Temptation has been with us ever since Adam and Eve were tempted to go against God's will in the Garden of Eden. I would have to address the consequences of their giving in to that temptation in another writing. Suffice to say for now that as a result, *death entered the world and trials and tribulations now abound.*

Christ himself had to be driven into the wilderness for forty days to be tempted to go against God's purpose for Him. Imagine the consequences from that if He had succumbed to those temptations! He endured those temptations as a man to show us we could overcome Satan's attempt to pull us away from our relationship with the Lord. Christ's experience in the wilderness is the ultimate meaning of *"no temptation has come to us that has not been experienced by others."*

He is our way of escape! If we keep our focus on Him and not the things that tempt us, He gives us the desire to overcome those temptations and to stay true to what we profess as a Christian. A marriage is a perfect example. If a husband or wife has the temptation to be unfaithful it will ultimately be their love for their partner that will keep them from the temptation and keep them true to the marriage. If our focus drifts from our loved one to anything else, the odds are relatively high that we will give in to the temptation. It is our love and dedication to Christ that provides our way of escape from temptations in life. What those temptations are will be different for each of us. Satan looks for the weak areas of our lives and that is where he will attack us.

I conclude with the same invitation that I gave to the person who requested that I address these Scriptures on temptation. I hope I have done justice to the question about what these passages mean. I am always available to discuss this or any other questions you may have regarding the Bible and our relationship with Christ. I consider it an honor.

Chapter 29
Shine Brightly for Christ

You are the light of the world-like a city on a hilltop that cannot be hidden. No one lights a lamp and then puts it under a basket. Instead, a lamp is placed on a stand, where it gives light to everyone in the house. In the same way, let your good deeds shine out for all to see, so that everyone will praise your Heavenly Father. " (Matthew 5: 14-16).

When we accept Jesus Christ into our lives He changes us. Our desires, our priorities, as well as our behavior undergo a massive transition. The things that are important to God become important to us. It starts with a desire to please Him, and whenever we fail at that we feel a sense of sadness that we have let Him down. It causes our language to change and our concern for our fellow man, especially the lost becomes a priority in our lives. Even our countenance changes. People may not know what has happened to us, but they see the change. This is what Matthew meant when he said, *"our light is like a city on a hilltop that cannot be hidden".* When we have sincerely accepted Christ into our lives it becomes very obvious. The Apostle Paul stated it this way, *"This means that anyone who belongs to Christ has become a new person. The old life is gone; a new life has begun."* (2 Corinthians 5:17).

If none of these attributes are present in our lives, the reason most likely is because we haven't truly surrendered our life and our will to Him. I have stated before that these changes are not something I work at doing because I have to as a Christian. They happen naturally as a result of Christ living in me.

When Christ left this world and returned to His Heavenly Father, He charged you and I with the responsibility of being the light (His light) in a dark and evil world. This should cause us to stop and think about the awesome responsibility that is, and that He is counting on us to now fulfill the purpose of His coming in the first place. We are His only example of who He is. Do you understand how heavy that is. If our life does not line up with His, we are in essence misrepresenting Him. I cannot think of any sin that is more egregious than misrepresenting God to be something He is not. Satan has used this one sin to turn people away from God more than anything else. If we misrepresent the truth by lying, if we become angry and lose control, if we use vulgar and off the wall language, it is not just a reflection on you and your character, it is a misrepresentation of who God is living within you. When the old things have not passed away it sends the message that God is not who He claimed to be and that His power is too weak to bring change in our lives. They see Him as not able to be their very present help in times of trouble. Unable or not caring enough to hear and answer our prayers. Too bankrupt to supply all our needs according to His riches and glory. Let me state this clearly, when we misrepresent who God is, it has eternal consequences. Our lives will either draw people to Christ, or repel them away from Him. *"Verily I say unto you, whatsoever ye shall bind on earth shall have been bound in heaven, and whatsoever you shall loose on earth will be loosed in heaven."* (Matthew 18:18 KJV).

The light that shines within us causes us to be stable whenever trouble surrounds us. While others may be frantic and living with heavy concern or fear, we are steadfast knowing that Christ is in control, and nothing can come my way that He is not aware of. When David penned the 23rd Psalm his light was shining bright when he testified that even while passing through the valley of the shadow of death He did not fear, because God was with Him. Paul affirmed it when he wrote in Romans 14:8 *"whether we live or die, we belong to the Lord."* These men had real encounters with the Lord and their lights shined brightly as a result.

What light do people see when they look into your life? Is it one that shines brightly and draws people in to want to know about this God living within you. Or is it a light that burns dimly and does not produce enough light for others to see their way to an all powerful God. How brightly your light shines really does matter in the light of eternity, not just for others but for you as well.

Chapter 30
He Knows You by Name

"Do not be afraid, for I have ransomed you. I have called you by name; You are mine" (Isaiah 43:1).

We live in a modern world where we are surrounded by people. Wherever we go we are never alone, or so it would seem. A quick trip to the store to pick up a few things and we stand in line with other people doing the same thing. Go to any mall to shop and there are people everywhere doing the same thing. All of us having the same habits, the same needs for food, clothing, or maybe entertainment. It's called human nature.

I used to travel a lot in my ministry. It seemed I spent more time in airports and on planes than I spent in my own home. I would sit in the waiting area of my gate with 150 other people waiting to board the same flight as myself. We would all board at the same time, find our seats and off we would go. All of us, heading in the same direction, at the same time, and the same destination. Yet with all this in common, we rarely spoke, did not know each other by name, and certainly knew absolutely nothing about each other.

Even surrounded by people on all sides, by neighbors and many times family members, we can feel invisible and very much misunderstood. Although there are so many people all around us, we fear sharing our inner most thoughts with others thinking we will be misunderstood, judged, and even shut out by others.

Do you know that feeling I am talking about? Have you been the one who was never invited with the other employees to lunch? Were you the one who felt left out of the clique at school? Even well-meaning church people are guilty of this sometimes. I lived in a part of the country where it was tradition to either have people over for Sunday dinner or go out for lunch after the service. But it was always the same people going together and the same people every Sunday going home without an invitation. Heaven help us if visitors came to church and expected an invite into that group invitation. My point to all of this is to simply say, we can live surrounded by people and yet be very much alone.

But there is good news! God, the Creator of the universe, knows you by name. With hundreds of millions of people throughout the world, He knows you by name. He knows you so personally that if a hair falls from your head to the ground, He knows about it before it even hits the floor (Matthew 10:30). You cannot have a thought, or a feeling of loneliness without His knowing and understanding what you are experiencing. He will never shut you out, exclude you, or make you feel rejected by Him. As a matter of fact, here is the rest of what He had to say to you in His own words right after He says He knows you by name: *"When you go through deep waters, I will be with you. When you go through rivers of difficulty you will not drown. When you walk through the fire of oppression, you will not be burned up; the flames will not consume you, for I am the Lord your God!"* With Him we are never alone.

Chapter 31
Describe Yourself in One Word

"I have told you these things so that you will be filled with my joy" (John 15:11).

I am blessed to have the best mother-in-law that a man could ask for. She respects me for the person I try to be, tells me often how glad she is that I am married to her daughter, and has made me feel as if I am a part of the family and not just a son-in-law. Recently she called me, and I could hear a little excitement in her voice. She wanted to share with me this new devotional she signed up for through guidepost called *Mornings with Jesus*. She wanted to know if she could share them with me when she was done with each month's edition. I was honored that she thought of me and wanted to share in her own spiritual journey. So, the following thoughts are from the one I read this morning, and Mom, this is for you.

I am not quite sure why the author chose this particular Scripture, but I did not change it to be true to her devotion. The author of this devotion started off by asking those who were reading this to do something. She asked that you write down the first word, and one word only, that you would like to pass on to others. She then went on to say that she chose the word *hope*. No one could deny this is certainly something that is fading at a rapid pace from the face of the earth. If we look through a practical lens, instead of things getting better, they are getting worse. People no longer care for each other as they should. We are faced with the reality of pandemics, world famine, as well as floods, earthquakes, and more. With the rapid decline in influence that God's people, the Church is having throughout the world, hope is certainly needed. Our world needs the hope that Christ promises when He says, *"I am the light of the world. If you follow me, you won't have to walk in darkness, because you will have the light that leads to life"* (John 8:12).

STOP! Do not read further yet. Well, read this then stop. Find a pencil and piece of paper and write down one word that describes what you would want to pass on to the world. I am going to wait five minutes before I begin again so you don't feel rushed....

Okay. Time is up.

This is where the author drew me in. I couldn't think of just one word without wanting to add the why behind it. Then, my mind drifted, as it does that a lot, and I began to think of the one word that I wanted to be remembered for when my time here is up. That wasn't any easier. I found a different word for different people or circumstances. What would my one word be for God, that was different from what I wanted my family to remember me for, and yet another word for those whom I have had the honor to have influence their lives? I couldn't arrive at a one-word answer in five minutes. It has now been about eighteen hours since I started my five-minute hourglass for myself. Finally, I arrived at the one word that I would like to pass on to the world, and at the same time be remembered for. That word was *faithful*.

Now before I go any further, I must give full disclosure on my faithfulness. This is something that at times in my life I have failed miserably to do. I have been a huge failure to God at times. I have failed my wife, my children, and even some who God placed in my life, trusting me to help them in their spiritual journey. Remember that the question was, *what one word do you want to be remembered for, or to pass on to the world?*

Here is just a snapshot of the things I thought about when trying to decide what I wanted that one word to be. I will limit it to just a summary of my thoughts on the word faithful as I am confident you don't want the whole eighteen hours. First, the Bible tells us that *"without faith, it is impossible to please God"* (Hebrews 11:6.) Since I want nothing more than to know my life pleases God, I chose *faith*. Secondly, the Bible tells us that if we just *"had the faith of a mustard seed we could move mountains"* (Matthew 17:20). I sincerely want the world to have the hope the author spoke of here. I want my family to know that there is hope for us as a family. I want those of you who read to know that there is hope for you and your family. We must choose to live by this faith because the Bible tells us that, *"by faith we are saved through His grace"* (Ephesians 2:8). I want you to experience that kind of faith that gives you His saving grace.

Now, one more question. "What one word do you think Christ would choose to pass on to the world. This is a no brainer for me. That word would absolutely be *love*! *"No greater love has any man than to lay down His life for His friends"* (John 15:13). Whether you realize it or not, He is your friend and He laid down His life just for you. Finally: *"For God so loved the world that He gave His only Son that whoever believed (had faith) in Him would not be condemned but through Him would be saved"* (John 3:16).

Pass it on!!!

Chapter 32
"It is Finished"… But We Have Only Just Begun

"I have been given all authority in heaven and on earth. Therefore, GO and make DISCIPLES of all the nations, BAPTIZING them in the name of Father, and the Son, and the Holy Spirit. Teach these new DISCIPLES to OBEY all the commands I have given you. And be sure of this, I am with you always, even to the end of the age." (Matthew 28: 18-20).

I have struggled finding just the right words so that it would be understood by everyone who reads this and not just those who are full-time Christian workers. We *all* have a role to play in this one. I am convinced that the condition of our world today is in most part a result of us as Christians either not understanding this, or out of complacency failing to fulfill our role. This one is most likely going to cause you to have questions, and hopefully challenge you to discover your real purpose in following Jesus. If that is the case with you, I pray you will privately message me or call me to talk about it.

I believe that I have made this statement before, but since these are the last words of Jesus here on earth, it is vital we understand the weight they carry. When a person comes to the end of their life on this earth, their thoughts and focus comes from somewhere deep within their heart and mind. We are not interested in what is for dinner tonight, or what I might wear to church next Sunday. We want to speak to the issues of the heart. Our love for our family, our hope for their future. Now here they are, the last words of Jesus. Someone in your life is counting on you to get this right. Their future, their eternity, is dependent not upon a pastor or priest, but upon your response to this *Great Commission*.

To be concise and not lose you, let's focus on the four commands within Jesus last statement, 1) *"Go," 2) "make disciples," 3) "baptize,"* and, *4) "teach them to obey."*

1). Go. The translation of *"Go"* from the original Greek is *"as you are going."* In other words, as you are living out your life at home, at work, and at play. For the Christian, our purpose in living out our faith is based on this foundational principle of a constant state of *going.* In case you think this is just directed to pastors or missionaries let me share the words of David in the 107th Psalm: *"Give thanks to the Lord, for He is good. His faithful love endures forever (v.1). Has the Lord redeemed you? Then speak out! Tell others He has redeemed you" (v.2).* And the last verse of the Psalm, *"those who are wise will take this to heart. They will see in our history the faithful love of our Lord" (v. 43).* Packed in the Psalm between verses 2 and 43, David reminds the people over and over of the times God showed up to meet their needs, deliver them from enemies, and give them food to eat and water to drink. Simply put, he is taking inventory of the goodness of God toward His people to say, share this message of God's goodness with others to show your gratitude and so others can experience it with you. Now turn back to these verses in Matthew 28. We too have been given many blessings throughout our life just as David's people. But we have been given far more than that through God's Son. Eternal life. Now instead of David speaking, it is Christ himself. The command is the same but more detailed. The message to us is still *speak out* with specific instructions. If we have been redeemed Christ is asking us to then make disciples.

2). Make disciples. These are the most important two words in these verses. A dear friend and fellow "disciple-maker, Dr. Ed Gross wrote a book entitled, "Are You a Christian or a Disciple?" In it he states, "words matter." We have a history of changing the original meaning of words over time. For example, in the Bible when it refers to being *gay,* it meant being happy. Today it means a sexual preference. I was educated in a rather conservative denomination that had a manual of denominational beliefs. The manual was written in 1904. In it were instructions that members do not attend the theater. 1904 was before the time of movie theatres. It was referring to such things as plays or burlesque and not films. What does all this have to do with the Great Commission? Apparently, everything. We have interchanged the word *disciple* for Christian. A disciple, when Jesus used the word, was someone who obediently followed his Rabbi (teacher). A disciple went wherever the Rabbi went, did everything the Rabbi commanded, and never questioned why. By today's definition, you can claim to be a disciple or Christian and never follow Jesus at all. We have drifted so far from the definition of disciple that to even suggest being obedient to the Rabbi, in this case Jesus, you are labelled as a fanatic. Nowhere in Scripture does it say we are to be just Christians, at least by today's definition. Jesus himself referred to us as followers. A follower would be someone who *follows* Him. To follow would mean to be in obedience to the one being followed, or in this case a disciple. I would need several more pages to fully explain making a *disciple*. Hopefully, we have addressed the minimum of going to *make disciples* by Jesus' definition.

3). Baptize. This one is pretty self-explanatory. I am tempted to tackle the subject of what Christian baptism is, but it would lead us down another path. I will save that one for another day. If you are reading this and you have never been baptized, I encourage you to do so. Since it was a direct command of Jesus and He Himself saw the importance of it to the extent that He Himself was baptized. If we sincerely want to be a follower of Christ this is where it starts.

4). Teach them to obey. There is that horrible word again…obey. God has expected obedience from us ever since the creation of Adam and Eve. We first see it in Genesis 2:15-17 when he warned Adam and Eve to *"not eat from the tree of knowledge of good and evil."* From that time on in both the Old and New Testament, the

141

foundational principle of following God is rooted in obedience. Now before you call me on the carpet about being saved by grace, I am not saying that obedience is what saves us. Only God's grace through His Son's death can do that. Obedience then, is our response to that grace. Obedience is called for as our response to grace over and over in the New Testament. Verses such as John 10:27: *"My sheep here my voice, and they FOLLOW me."* John 14:15: *"If you love me, keep my commandments,* and 1John 2:3: *"And we can be sure that we know Him if we OBEY His commandments."* Over and over from Genesis through Revelation the Bible cries out for obedience to the Father.

So, what is the point of all this? First, if this was truly the most important thing that Christ was leaving with us, we need to take it seriously. Secondly, it is the calling of every Christian/disciple to obey. It is our failure to understand this that is keeping the Great Commission from being fulfilled today. Think about this, if those eleven men had failed to obey Christ and meet him on the hill that day to hear His parting words, Christianity would have died in that moment. Our failure to understand our role in obedience has all but rendered us impotent!

Instead of seeing obedience as a radically negative thing, embrace it as an act of love to the one who gave His life for you. There is someone out there, most likely several some ones, who are counting on you to get it right and their eternal future hangs in the balance.

Chapter 33
Focus

"You stubborn people! You are heathen at heart and deaf to the truth. Must you forever resist the Holy Spirit? That's what your ancestors did, and so do you! Name one prophet your ancestors didn't persecute! They even killed the ones who predicted the coming of the Righteous One – the Messiah whom you betrayed and murdered. You deliberately disobeyed God's law, even though you received it from the hand of angels" (Acts 7: 51-56 NLT).

The Jewish leaders were infuriated by Stephen's accusations, and they shook their fist at him in rage. But Stephen, full of the Holy Spirit, gazed steadily into heaven and saw the glory of God, and he saw Jesus standing in the place of honor at God's right hand. He told them: *Look, I see the heavens open and the Son of man standing in the place of honor at God's right hand!"* Then they put their hands over their ears and began shouting. They rushed at him and dragged him out of the city and began to stone him. His accusers took off their coats and laid them at the feet of a young man named Saul. As they stoned him, Stephen prayed, Lord Jesus, receive my spirit. He fell to his knees shouting, "Lord, don't charge them with this sin!" With that, he died.

A few months ago, I had a conversation with a close friend. As we talked, he made the statement, "I want to walk so close to God that I always know what His will is for me, and I can hear Him when He desires to speak to me." That statement would not leave me that day as I drove an hour and fifteen minutes home. Is it possible that we can walk so close to God that no matter what is going on around us we can recognize His presence in our lives? Before you dismiss that thought as wishful thinking, I challenge you to look into this passage of Scripture of Stephen's final moments on earth. I will explain why in a moment, but I believe that next to the death of Christ on the Cross, Stephen's death just might have been the second most important death in Christianity.

Can you imagine the uproar in the Western World if Stephen was speaking to the church with those words today? In a society today that gets angry over the simplest of testimony that we are Christians, it is not a stretch for me to believe that at a minimum, he would be arrested for inciting a riot or accused of hate speech.

I also wonder if there were those who assumed God would protect him for his bold stand that ultimately questioned *where was God* when Stephen seemed to need Him the most? And what about Stephen? Did he wonder where God was during those last moments before he drew his last breath? The Scripture seems to indicate that those kinds of thoughts were far from his mind. He was focused, not on things of this world, but on things of Heaven - focused on God.

To say that Stephen had succeeded in making them angry would be an understatement. They were enraged to the point of wanting him dead. How dare he judge them for their piousness? He had called them out for their hypocrisy, and it struck a nerve. And Stephen realized he was about to die. Instead of turning and running away or screaming out "why Lord?" he was focused; so focused that he could gaze into the sky and see heaven open. There was Jesus, not sitting but standing looking back at Stephen. Jesus recognized the importance of what was taking place to the point of rising to His feet as He watched it unfold. I hope to ask Stephen one day, "what were you thinking when you saw Jesus standing there?" I can tell from the text that he wasn't thinking "why Lord?" Stephen was laser focused with his eyes locked on Jesus for what was to come next.

They dragged him out of the city and began to stone him. They would not stop until his body lay lifeless in the street. Yet, even as the pain of the stones crashed upon the side of his head, not even this could shake his focus. He cried out: *"Lord, receive my spirit,"* followed by words that I am not sure I could have spoken at the time: *"Father, do no charge them with this sin!"*

Stephen never lost his focus on what mattered. Being so close to God that no matter what may come, he would not lose heart. He would not allow his faith to be shaken. Oh, that I could someday have that kind of focus. To be so close to God that no matter what life throws at me; to see heaven opened and Christ standing, (not sitting,) proud of my faith in the one who gave His life for me.

I started this devotion by saying that next to Christ' death on the Cross, Stephen's death might be the second most important death in the Christian world. Present that day was a devout member of that high court that put Stephen to death. His name was Saul. He was so honored for his aggression against Christians that when they killed Stephen, they took their coats and laid them at Saul's feet. Saul no doubt saw the look on Stephen's face as he gazed up to heaven and looked into the eyes of Jesus. A look of peace and not fear or doubt. He heard Stephen offer his spirit up to Jesus and then asked that Saul and his religious friends not be held accountable for what they had done.

This was the same Saul that shortly after would meet face to face with Jesus on the way to persecute other Christians in the same manner as Stephen was persecuted. That meeting would turn out to be the catalyst for spreading the gospel throughout the entire world. As a result of witnessing Stephen's death, his laser focus on Jesus, Saul knew who was confronting him that day. It was the same Jesus that Stephen saw standing at the right hand of God, and Saul acknowledged Him as Lord: *"'Who are you, Lord?' Saul asked. 'I am*

Jesus, whom you are persecuting,' he replied" (Acts 9:5). Without the death of Stephen, there would not have been a Saul who became Paul the Apostle. Without Paul there would not have been a missionary journey that spread Christianity throughout the world.

It was all part of God's plan. Stephen was focused on what mattered that day. Instead of trying to *figure it out*, he leaned into God and was honored by a standing Savior who cheered him on. As a result, you and I can know Christ to the same depth as Stephen.

What will be our focus as we face the challenges of life here on earth? May it be said of me that in those times of darkness and despair, I am so focused that I can look up at heaven and see Christ standing (not sitting,) cheering me on, and proud of me for my faith and love for Him.

Chapter 34
What Really Matters

"Every time I think of you, I give thanks to my God. Whenever I pray, I make my requests for all of you with joy, for you have been my partners in spreading the Good News about Christ from the time you first heard it until now." …So, it is right that I should feel as I do about all you, for you have a special place in my heart."…God knows how much I love you and long for you with the tender compassion of Christ Jesus. I pray that your love will overflow more and more, and that you will keep on growing in knowledge and understanding. For I want you to understand <u>what really matters</u>, so that you may live pure and blameless lives until the day of Christ's return" (Philippians 1: 3-5, 7-10 NLT).

It doesn't take more than a cursory look at Paul's letter to the Philippians to realize that they had a special place in his heart. His opening remarks come across with a very intimate tone. It was important to him that he express his deep love for them and what they had come to mean to him in his own personal life.

That has caused me to reflect on my own journey through life and how so many have influenced my walk with the Lord throughout the years. As a result, before we take a deep look at what really matters to all of us in light of eternity, I want to take Paul's personal approach, and reach out to all of you who are reading this now.

Those of you who know me personally may not think that you have had any influence upon my life. You would be wrong in that knowing you has helped to shaped me into the person I strive to be. As I have meditated on these passages, so many of you have come across my mind. Not just those with whom I have had long-standing relationship, but many who have crossed my path for just moments in my life. If you are reading this, then you can pretty much be assured that you are counted among those special people. You have added value to my life, and as a result I have felt this strong obligation to live my life in such a way that it would bring value to yours. At a minimum, I felt I needed to live in such a way that gave you no doubt that my experience with the Lord was real and that it would at least give you pause to believe it could be real for you as well.

I keep a running list in my phone of people I pray for every day, usually between three and five am. Again, if we are connected through Facebook, worked together, worshipped together, or been neighbors, you most likely are, or have been on that list. Many of you are on it right now and your name was lifted to the Creator just this morning. The affect that it has on me when I lift you up in prayer is that I sincerely thank God for you every time I speak your name before the Lord.

What are those things that should really matter to us in light of our existence here on earth as well as eternity? The first one should be obvious. At the top of what matters should be where we plan to spend eternity. We live in a time in America where many assume that everyone goes to heaven no matter how they have lived their lives. Almost without exception, when someone dies, I hear the phrase, *they are in a better place.* To challenge that statement in the midst of a families' grief would be cruel and come across extremely insensitive. So let me do it here, hopefully in a non-threatening and respectful way. It is so true that God loves us each and everyone. It was for that very reason He sent His Son to die a sinner's death on the Cross so that you and I could live with Him eternally. But it requires a response on our part. It is like receiving an invitation with a RSVP to an important function. Several years ago, I received such an invitation to an event hosted at the White House by then President George W. Bush. Upon arrival I discovered several people who were being turned away because they had failed to return the RSVP.

Because they failed to return the RSVP no background check was performed.

In Matthew 7:21, Jesus makes this statement: *"not everyone who calls me 'Lord, Lord!' shall enter the Kingdom of Heaven but he that does the Will of the Father."* That is our response to His RSVP. In light of Jesus RSVP invitation, it really matters how we respond. Where we will spend eternity depends upon it.

In the opening chapter on Legacy, I referred to a poem about the *Dash in the Middle.* The point of the poem is that it matters how we spend our time here on earth. Did it even matter that I was here?

I have thought a lot about this lately. As I am laid to rest will it be said that I was a good husband? Did my presence in the marriage make me a better person? Was I the kind of marriage partner that my wife was proud of? That matters to me.

It matters to me what kind of father I was. An old friend from years ago once said to me, "Richard, the best gift you will ever give your children is a Christian father." Did I deliver on that? Did my role as a father, model that of our heavenly Father? Anything short of that would be an absolute failure. That matters to me. Finally, what about the world around me? Did I have any impact on my co-workers? Was I a good neighbor that would make them at least consider this Jesus I proclaim? That matters to me.

Enough about me. What are those things that matter to you? I pray that at the top of your list, knowing Jesus in a personal way is covered. It is not enough to know about Him. That matters to Him!

Chapter 35
Things that Accompany Salvation

"The thief does not come except to steal, and to kill, and to destroy. I have come that they may have life, and that they may have it more abundantly" (John 10:10 NKJV).

In my youth there were many preachers and evangelists that tried to scare the living hell out of people. While it is true that hell is a literal place where those who reject Christ go, it is my belief that this is the wrong premise for accepting Christ.

I just watched a documentary on shark attacks tonight. Not what I would have chosen for entertainment, but my wife and grandson were really into it, so I joined in watching the program. Just for the record, when the program ended, I remarked, "now you know why I don't swim in the ocean." There was one part of this documentary that has inspired me to write this chapter. It illustrates why I think you should consider giving your heart and life to Jesus Christ rather than having hell scared out of you. A father was swimming with his daughter and her friend off the coast of New Zealand when the dad spotted a great white shark swimming directly toward them. Not wanting to alarm the girls as they were all swimming to shore, he placed himself between the shark and the girls. He realized that his life was about to be over, but the life of his daughter would be sparred along with that of her friend. I believe that most people would have shouted out "shark!" and hoped that they could all reach the shore safely. This father was not going to leave that to chance. The lives of those two girls could not be left to chance. The only way to be assured of their safety would be to stand between them and the shark. Would you not agree that this must be one of the most heroic things a father could do for his child?

This is exactly what Christ has done for you and me. I have no doubt that those two young girls who were saved from the shark have a special place in their heart for what that man did. Christ gave up His life for mankind even though He knew that there would be those who would reject and despise Him. I think of this every time someone denies His existence to me, or someone who uses His name in vain. He loved you and me so much that even knowing there would be people who would reject Him, He died anyway. If you truly understand the depth of His love for you, the next time you read John 3:16, it should have a deeper meaning to you: *"For God so loved the world that He gave His only son so that whosoever would believe in Him would be saved."* That is what should motivate you and I to want to believe in and follow Him and not just for the selfish reason of escaping hell.

In addition, I am hoping that by now you understand that accepting Christ as Savior is not the end of the journey but just the beginning. There is still a life to be lived here on earth either until He calls us home, or He makes His return to gather us all who have put their faith and trust in Him.

God wants us to live this life in the abundance of His love. Again, like those hellfire and brimstone preachers of old, we have a generation of preachers today that preach an unbiblical gospel of health and wealth. They will tell you that if you are living in the will of God, you will never be sick, and riches will flow your way. I find this to be not only wrong but cruel. I have watched many of these services where truly sick and disabled people leave the services still disabled and sick. These so-called faith healers blame it on the lack of faith on the part of the individual. I need to stop here before I go off on topic and tell you how I really feel about those who prey on the vulnerable.

The type of abundance Christ is speaking of in John 10 is far more than just temporal things. It is a type of abundance that rises above wealth and health. Ever since sin entered the world bad things happen in life that we simply cannot control. They will continue until such a time as Christ returns to restore what was taken away in the Garden of Eden. The abundance Christ offers is the ability to rise above those things with peace and confidence that God has us in the palm of His hand. I think of Joni Erikson who was paralyzed in a diving accident so many years ago. From her wheelchair, she has testified of God's love for her for over fifty years now. She would be the first to tell you that she knows what abundant living in Christ is all about. Then there was Corrie Ten Boom who survived the Holocaust and lived for a while in a Nazi concentration camp. Horratio Spafford wrote these words to the song *It is Well with My Soul* after losing his daughters at sea, "When peace like a river attendeth my way, when sorrows like sea billows roll, whatever my lot, thou has taught me to say, it is well, it is well with my soul." All these people and countless others understand the meaning behind Christ's promise to give us an abundant life. His grace is more than sufficient, it is abundant. His love for you is abundant. He gives to anyone who wants to receive it, the faith to overcome any trial that life throws our way. Here is the Scripture that comes to my mind when I think of God's abundance: *"What then shall we say to these things? If God is for us who can be against us? He who did not spare His own Son, but delivered Him up for us all, how shall He not with Him also freely give us all things? Who shall bring a charge against God's elect? It is God who justifies. Who is he who condemns? It is Christ who died, and furthermore is also risen, who is even at the right hand of God, who also makes intercession for us. Who shall separate us from the love of Christ? Shall tribulation, or distress, or persecution, or famine, or nakedness, or peril, or sword? As it is written, 'For your sake we are killed all day long. We are counted as sheep for the slaughter. Yet in all these things we are more than conquerors through Him who loved us. For I am persuaded that neither death, nor life, nor angels, nor principalities, nor powers, nor things present, nor things to come, nor height, nor depth, nor any other creature shall be able to separate us from the love of God which is in Christ Jesus our Lord"* (Romans 8:31-39)! This is the abundant living which God offers to each and everyone of us who put our faith and trust in Him.

Hopefully, we have scratched the surface about the things that accompany salvation. Christ came for far more than just to forgive us of our sins. He came to give us life and to give it to us abundantly. It is available to you right here and right now. All the money and wealth cannot buy what Christ offers to you. 1 Peter 5:7 tells us: *"Cast your care upon Him, for He cares for you."* In another Scripture Jesus made this statement: *"So if the Son sets you free, you are truly free"* (John 8:36 NLT).

Cast your cares upon Him and be set free to enjoy a life that accompanies salvation.

Chapter 36
The Last Season...
The Reality of Heaven

"Don't let your hearts be troubled. Trust in God and trust also in me. There is more than enough room in my Father's home. If this were not so, would I have told you that I am going to prepare a place for you? When everything is ready, I will come and get you; so that you will always be with Me where I am. And you know the way to where I am going." (John 14:1-4)

"I heard a shout from the throne, saying, Look, God's home is now among His people! He will live with them, and they will be His people. God himself will be with them. He will wipe away every tear from their eyes, and there will be no more death or sorrow or crying or pain. All these things are gone forever" (Revelation 21: 3-4).

Jesus has spent three years with these disciples. They had shared good times as well as bad times together. They were together around the clock. They traveled together, shared meals together, and slept on the hard ground together. These were men that Jesus came to love dearly. Realizing that His capture and crucifixion is just hours away, He is preparing His disciples for His impending death. These verses in John 14 were so profoundly comforting that we still repeat them today every time a loved on dies. Christ is making a solemn vow to them, as well as to you and me. That vow is for those who share in the kind of relationship He had with these men He had come to love. It was genuine, it was deep, and it was very personal. That is what it means to be a Christ follower.

Almost 100 years after that day, Jesus gives us a deeper look at what is to come. Once again it is very deep, and it is very personal. Can you imagine what it would feel like to have the hand of God to touch your cheek? To feel the warmth of that touch. To feel the power and strength that flows through the hand of God. Not only is it personal and deep, it is also intimate. That is what it means to have a personal relationship with Jesus Christ. It is certainly not about a religious routine. It is much more personal than that.

A very close friend recently shared these thoughts with me on Matthew 7:21-23 which reads (in part) *"Not everyone who calls out to me Lord, Lord will enter the Kingdom of Heaven...On judgement day many will say to me, Lord, Lord! We prophesied in your name, and cast out demons in your name and performed many miracles in your name. But I will reply (said Jesus),I never knew you."*

They called Him Lord, they spoke of things to come (prophesied) in His name, they did all the good things that Christians do, BUT THEY NEVER KNEW HIM! There are millions of churchgoers today that do all the good things that Christians do. They attend church, they sing in the choir or are on the worship team, they even pay their tithe, but they have never experienced a personal and intimate relationship with Him. That is what He wants. It is what He has always wanted since creating Adam and Eve. Listen to just some of the excerpts from Isaiah 1 *"what makes you think I want all your sacrifices?... "When you come to worship Me, who asked you to parade through my courts with all your ceremony?... stop bringing me your meaningless gifts,... They are a burden to me."* This is just a sampling of what God had to say in these verses about the exercise of religion. These things are not bad. In fact, they are very, very good. But void of a personal relationship with God, they mean nothing to Him. It is about the relationship and not the works.

Earlier in this book we talked about the seasons of life. The final season comes for all of us. Life has taught me that the final season is not defined by how many years we have on earth. I have preached the funeral of a newborn infant, of a teenaged girl, and responded to a mass shooting at a high school where both students and teachers alike died. The last season of life is inevitable and it will not be about what you did, it will be about who you know.

There is another old hymn we used to sing when I was a child. The words of the chorus said, "Jesus, oh Jesus, do you know Him today, please don't turn Him away,

Oh Jesus, my Jesus, without Him how lost I would be."

So how do you get to know Him? How do you go from a religious experience to a personal relationship with Him? It really is quite simple. You do what those disciples did who were with Jesus during His time on earth. They walked with Him, they ate meals with Him, wherever He went they followed. They shared life together. That is how you get to know Him. There is a cliché that I often hear quoted that says, "It isn't what you know but who you know that counts." Never is it more true than in having a personal relationship with Jesus Christ.

When finally that last season of life comes, if you truly know Him, if you have repented of your sin and turned to Him, if you have that personal relationship with Him, you will be with Him forever and there will be no more heartache, no more pain, no more sickness, no more death. Instead you will feel the warmth and power of the hand of God as He places it on your cheek, and all the worries will be over.